Driving with Cats:
Ours for a Short Time

Driving with Cats:
Ours for a Short Time

Catherine Holm

NORTH STAR PRESS OF ST. CLOUD, INC.
St. Cloud, Minnesota

To Chris, who helps make it all possible,
and to all my animal teachers, past, present, and future.

Deep gratitude to Betty Vos for initial editing of this manuscript,
A.J. for many years of writing fellowship and guidance,
all my veterinarians and their dedicated staff for their above-and-
beyond support (Dr. Chip, Dr. Sue, Dr. John, and Dr. Ralph),
my husband for his unfailing support,
and everyone who has ever encouraged me on the creative path.

First edition: June 1, 2013

Printed in the United States of America

Published by
North Star Press of St. Cloud, Inc.
P.O. Box 451
St. Cloud, MN 56302

www.northstarpress.com   Facebook - North Star Press   Twitter - North Star Press

Contents

Introduction

*I*AM DEFINED BY MY CATS.

In an earlier stage of life, I may have been ashamed to admit this, but no more! This is one of the benefits of growing older. We care less what people think. That's a good thing, and quite freeing.

My cats have become a huge part of my life and yes, they have come to define me. Though I didn't realize it until a few years ago, it is no accident my first name contains the syllable "Cat." I have started going by "Cat," which I prefer to "Catherine."

How have my cats come to define me? I have had cats since 1989, when I adopted two Humane Society refugees to celebrate breaking up with an alcoholic boyfriend. (He was a nice guy with a lot of problems.) Adopting these cats represented a life milestone—I honored my new freedom.

A year later I met Chris, the man I would marry. Chris has been a big part of my life with cats, and I think the cats have defined him as well. Never believe a person who says they don't like cats. A cat can and often will break into and enter the most doubtful heart.

My cats teach me daily lessons about joy, lightening up, having a sense of humor, patience, beauty, and loss. By the time I met my husband, I had already lost one of the original two cats that I adopted to celebrate my short life as a single person. But I could never guess at the cats that would follow. During the twenty-two years we've been together, we've had twelve cats and four dogs. Six cats and one dog are alive today. I do the best to give these animal companions wonderful, interesting lives, and they in turn make my life wonderful and interesting.

During the twenty-two years I've been with my husband and have shared our home with cats and dogs, our address has changed five times. The most dramatic move was from address number three (a small house in St. Paul, Minnesota) to address number four (a trailer in remote northern Minnesota). The cats gamely went along with the plan, and helped me with this life-changing adjustment. They were with me in a lonely new place as I went through severe culture shock in getting used to a remote rural area.

We've been at address number five now for seventeen years in the same remote rural area and we may or may not be here for good. The house is one story with no basement, and small by U.S. standards (800 square feet). I was raised with a compulsive ethic of cleanliness so I do my best to keep the house as clean as possible, even with several indoor cats. I've never had the courage to let the cats roam outside. There are plenty of predators here in the woods that would snap up a cat in no time.

Every morning, without fail, I clean four litter boxes. You should, the literature says, have a box for each cat. However, in our one-story log house, I only have room for four boxes. One box goes in the bathroom, three go behind the propane heater. I hope no one notices them too much.

Every morning and every evening I mix medicines for the cats. I probably go above and beyond what many people would do for their cats, and I have been doing it for years. They get immune-boosting supplements, liver support in one case for worrisome lab values, and anti-cancer holistic support for my young black cat who seems determined to grow lumps. If the lumps can grow, maybe they can just as easily dissolve away. That is my hope.

I have also spent many hours driving with cats. The drives are usually intense. I am being selfish; the drives are intense for me, not necessarily for the cats.

The cats are any color, any size or age. Tiny, fat, orange, tabby, silver, brown, white; long or short haired; eighteen years, ten years, two months. The cat may be squalling or may be a good, silent rider. We may be heading for a vet checkup, or to diagnose some worrisome development, or taking the most dreaded ride of all—euthanasia. These car rides are burned into my memory. Seared into my mind is a four-hour freeway ride to the cities with my black cat Target for risky surgery. Or a two-hour drive through snowstorms to an emergency vet with my streetsmart orange Milo. I live in the country and my favorite vets are either one hour away, or four hours away. The shorter drive is a two-lane highway through remote boreal forest. The four-hour drive is all freeway, and ends with the intense heat generated by the concrete of a large city. I've spent a lot of time driving with cats.

Sometimes the lessons are bitter and sweet. How to let go. How to be strong. How to serve. How to stay in the moment. How to love—with a depth I didn't know possible.

Losing my cats has been harder for me than losing the few people in my life to date. What does this say about me—that I love cats better than people? I don't think so. But perhaps cats unlock a piece of me that most people don't. I would like to be as unlocked with people as I am with cats. Maybe time is the requirement—perhaps in another thirty years I will grieve with the intensity for humans that I do for cats. I don't expect others to understand this—I only know that it is true. I grew up in a family where expressive love was not the norm. We were encouraged to be independent and get out on our own. I still carry the benefits and the snags of this upbringing—I don't play too well in groups and I have a hard time trusting.

But my cats I can trust. They give their love freely. When I am with cats, I interact with them in the same way that many people act around babies. I want to hold them, and I feel love warming my heart and spilling out into the world. I think it is safe to say cats have taught me how to love.

Most people in my life know of my enthusiasm for cats. These folks have begun to think of me as some kind of cat expert. They ask me how to deal with cat behavior issues. They wonder about various treatments. I am not a vet. They ask me to communicate with their cats.

I do not want that responsibility. I prefer, instead, to think of it this way: We all have the answers, we and our animals. There is intense and lovely communication that can go on between us, if we are open to it. There are no wrong answers. Our animals do not judge. Perhaps this is why the human/animal-companion bond can be so intense and rewarding. Perhaps this is why our animal family members can feel like life preservers in a world that seems like it might drown us, or at least toss us around. The constant love from my animal companions and the lessons they bring to my life has caused me to write this book.

Life is a journey; relationships are a journey. Driving is a literal journey from point A to point B. Relationships and life aren't always so direct or easy to traverse. Whether I am literally driving with my cats, or navigating some of the most courageous and loving and heartbreaking territory of my life with my cats, I am in awe of what they teach me. Many of you have deep and complex relationships with your animal companions as well, and I hope reading about my journeys with my cats will help you or touch your heart.

Rama (back) and Chester (front).
(Photo courtesy of the author.)

Note for Readers

THIS BOOK IS FRAMED with the story of my cat Jamie–the beginning, middle, and end of his life. In between the story of Jamie, I have interspersed my stories of other cats, my own story, and my thoughts on what animal companions can teach us.

Dogs have a special, growing place in my heart as well. (Thanks to the special and current dog teachers in my life: Corona, GusGus, and Walli!) This book focuses on cats simply because that's where I've had the most experience and time. I believe animal companions of any species are a huge blessing in our lives–they have surely enriched mine.

Tigger, one of my first cats.
(Courtesy of Deborah Sussex Photography.)

Cat Family Tree
(in order of adoption into our household)

Cleo: gray and white short-haired female, adopted 1989, died 1989.

Tigger: white-and-cream-colored long-haired female, adopted 1989, died 1999.

Jamie: orange medium-haired tabby male, adopted 1991, died 2011.

Milo: orange short-haired tabby male, adopted 1992, died 2007.

Karma: silver-and-brown short-haired Siamese and tabby female, rescued 1997.

Kali: black, brown, and white short-haired tabby female, adopted 1999.

Target: black short-haired male, adopted 2001, died 2007.

Rama: black short-haired male, adopted 2007.

Chester: orange short-haired tabby male, adopted 2007.

Kieran: white short-haired male (domestic with white-and-black Van pattern), rescued 2008.

Karma.
(Courtesy of Deborah Sussex Photography.)

Act I:
Jamie—The Beginning of the End

I WATCH MY CATS LIKE A MOTHER watches her children. When something is off, I notice immediately. So when I started noticing that Jamie, my twenty-year-old orange cat, was suddenly not eating, I was worried.

It was spring in northern Minnesota, a happy time. The snow was gone. Outdoor projects could be addressed for the house and our land. We were getting ready to put plant starts in the ground. My husband and I were outside all the time, an arrangement I loved. We'd already been into the Boundary Waters Canoe Area Wilderness once, in late April, because the ice had come off the lakes so early. Bad things were not supposed to happen in the spring. We don't expect them. But then, are we ever prepared for bad times?

"Chris, look at this," I called out to my husband. Our house was small with an open design. We could see everybody and everything, inside.

We watched Jamie. He was interested in food, and obviously hungry. He put his nose up to the dry kibble in a bowl, but he wouldn't take a bite. He pawed at the brown pellets, spilling them out of the bowl and onto the floor. Jamie had never been a fussy eater. He pawed at the water bowl, too. That'd always been his trick, but now, he was also not drinking the water.

You expect trouble with an older cat. Yet, unrealistically, I had forgotten that trouble could happen. This long-haired orange cat was strangely hardy for a cat who came from a pet store (and by association, probably came from a kitten mill). Jamie had a will of steel and it was my suspicion he'd lived so long because of that will. I needed him, I wanted him, to harness his willpower now.

I phoned the vet and that feeling that I'd come to know—when something was off with my cats—came back. It was a feeling of dread,

The Contents of My Cat Junk Drawer

My cat junk drawer includes:
- Six cat toothbrushes. I had grand plans to brush each cat's teeth daily, but have so far failed to make it a regular practice.
- One tube of cat toothpaste (yes, this is different from human toothpaste).
- A large broken flashlight (unrelated to cats).
- Several jingly balls (I only have the kind with hard exteriors where the cat cannot get at the jingle bell inside).
- A few stuffed mouse toys. I try to find ones that don't have appendages (eyes, ears, etc.) that the cats could chew off and swallow. I also try to find really sturdy ones that the cats can't chew apart (and eat the stuffing inside). I don't care for the really tiny mice, since they seem small enough for a cat with a large mouth to swallow.
- Three to four cat harnesses, and a long leash (lead). On nice summer days, I may bring the cats outside when I'm close by, but we don't have a fenced yard. Someday I'd love to make them a large outdoor pen/play area, but too many other homestead projects have taken priority. Someday!
- A feather duster with a long shoelace attached to it. The duster is chemical free. I drag it around on the floor and let the cats chase it. Strangely, they all seem to prefer chasing the shoelace rather than the feather end—probably because the shoelace moves more rapidly on the floor and provides more stimulation. Rama, a.k.a. Dyson, a.k.a. Pointy Paws, knows how to open the drawer and drag out the shoelace/duster toy. Smart cat!
- Supplement these toys with good food, fresh catnip from the garden, and lots of love, and I think these cats have a fine life.

like going down a dark chute into an abyss on the other side. I got an appointment for the next day—a one-hour drive one way to a town on the edge of the wilderness.

To the non-local eye, most of the region we live in looks like wilderness. As I drove, I forgot to be glad it was spring and that I wouldn't have to worry about icy roads, always a huge stressor. I was only worried about Jamie, and feared what the vet visit would uncover.

Jamie had some major hurdles in his life, but he was a tough cat and blazed through some pretty hairy situations. Chris and I adopted him shortly after we started living together. Early onset kidney disease was discovered when Jamie was about ten years old. We managed for many years with herbal supplements. When Jamie was sixteen, he was still jumping with ease from the kitchen counters to the "catwalk"—the tops of the kitchen cabinets. (I have never been able to train my cats to stay off counters.) When Jamie was eighteen, he got a herpes infection in an eye, and needed to have the eye removed. Any anesthesia and surgery is very risky for such an old cat—they may not wake up. But during the eye surgery, the vet tech told me Jamie's heart never stopped beating and never wavered.

2

It was one strong, steady sustained beat. I like to think Jamie's success through these risky surgeries and procedures had to do with his immensely strong will. Jamie always got what he wanted. Very little slowed him down.

The next day I woke up, fear and worry eating at the edges of my mind. I loaded Jamie into the carrier and put him on the passenger side of the bench seat of our small Toyota truck.

"It will be okay," said Chris. I wanted to believe it. I hoped so.

The hour-long drive to the vet's office was all two-lane, rural paved highway. The drive was nondescript until the twenty-mile mark. By then, I'd gone through Tower, a town that is the same size as my town. Between Tower and Ely, the road suddenly seemed more remote and wild. I associated the road to Ely with the Boundary Waters Wilderness, one of my favorite places. Ely is one way to enter the Boundary Waters.

Jamie sat next to me, in his carrier, quiet. He had always been a good rider. He was more fearless than I was.

The twenty-mile stretch of Highway 169 between Tower and Ely was curvy, a little hilly, and sparsely populated. The tires slapped rhythmically on the cracks in the road. This climate is hard on roads that have basically been built on swamps. Every year the frost heaves and the roads acquire new dips and swings.

I have driven this stretch many times in the winter, when you really have to watch the turns. Snow and ice form and melt unevenly on this road, given its east-west orientation, the lowness of the sun during the winter at these latitudes, and the shade of forest trees that often come right up to the shoulder of the road.

In June, I wasn't worrying about ice, but I was speeding at sixty miles per hour. This seemed to be the "safe" zone on a fifty-five mile per hour highway here, and I didn't push it. There was a part of me that wanted to drive fast out of nervousness, and there was a part of me that never wanted to arrive at the vet's office. I wanted to suspend myself and Jamie in time and space. I didn't want to find out what was on the other end of this. I wanted to keep Jamie forever and everything that was uniquely Jamie—the way he loved to ride on our shoulders, the way he fetched a ball when he was young and brought it back to us, dropping it at our feet each time, over and over and over. His long and silky fur. Even his persnickety personality. His passionate head butting—especially when he was in a room with us, alone. Jamie loved the times when he could feel as if he was the only cat, even though that was rarely possible in our household.

I passed a lone house on the left—firewood neatly stacked on the lot and ready for next winter; a small fenced garden that was ready for this year's seeds or seed starts. The house looked well-kept and organized. I was suddenly jealous of and irrationally angry at that peaceful-seeming abode. I wanted some peace instead of the worry that was stirring in my gut. Oblivious to or ignoring my worry, Jamie stared straight ahead. His fur, which had always required a lot of grooming, seemed to have recently developed more and more mats. We had to cut some of them out.

The vet began by looking at Jamie's teeth and found nothing. Then, he attempted to look under Jamie's tongue. This was not easily done as a cat's tongue sits low in the mouth. But a red mass under the tongue was visible.

The vet recommended putting Jamie under to get a better look at what was going on under the tongue. The mass looked like a possible laceration or a cancerous mass.

"If it's a cancerous mass," said the vet, "I recommend we don't wake him up."

The words electrified me. I had to hold onto the stainless vet examining table. Don't wake him up. I was going to be sick. No time for goodbyes? I'd never pictured this unpleasant ending. But do we ever picture the endings? My body stiffened with stress in this unreal moment. I tried to wrap my head around a response.

"Only if you're absolutely sure it is cancer," I finally stammered. I hated this awful predicament. Chris wouldn't even get to say goodbye! I prayed for a miracle—that the mass was not cancer, but possibly an infected cut.

JAMIE WAS IN A HOLDING ROOM at the vet's office, a small room with metal cages stacked two high, where cats and small dogs were either being kenneled or waiting for surgery. The vet's office was closed for the doctors' customary lunch break, but they let me stay behind and be with Jamie.

I didn't know whether to be saying goodbye or whether to reassure Jamie I'd be seeing him on the other end of this. I was a mess and I was shaking. This could be my last two hours with Jamie. I stood in front of his second-story cage, and I had the door open and my arm inside the cage. For two hours I stood here, crying, petting him, telling him every good thing I can think of.

"I love you. You're my Tuega! Ka-chuck-ah-chuck-ah-chuck!" "Tuega" was Jamie's nickname, but don't ask me what it derived from. "Ka-chuck-ah-chuck-ah-chuck" is a noise I made when Jamie rode my shoulders. He seemed to like it, or at least I told myself that. Don't ask me what any of these silly connections derive from. We created immense stories and trappings around our cats.

I loved him. I had entered nightmare territory—every pet owner's worst dream.

This situation reminded me of when Jamie had eye surgery two years prior. It was risky and dangerous. I dropped Jamie at the vet in the morning and waited several hours until I could pick him up, assuming he made it through the procedure. Since the vet was an hour from my home, I killed time in town. But I was worthless for conversation, reading, work, anything. I had many friends in Ely but I didn't let any of them know I was in town. I didn't think I could interact with a friend and not break down.

In the holding room, Jamie seemed grumpy, like he wanted to go home. I was trying desperately to hold onto every detail of him that I could, in case he didn't make it through the procedure or cancer was found. I felt the fine texture of Jamie's fur. I scratched his chin, telling him I loved him and wishing there was a way I could pour more love into each word. I looked into his one beautiful green eye. What if I never saw him again, alive? What if he didn't get told everything I wanted to tell him? I was crying, and my nose was sore from blowing it. I had to travel the following week for some expensive yoga training that was already paid for. How could I go out in the world? I just wanted to be with Jamie. I hated this moment; I wanted it over, and I dreaded it ending.

THERE WAS MORE DREAD for me as the door to the room opened and the vet and an assistant appeared. Again, I felt close to fainting. The vet and the tech seemed surprised I was still in the room.

"Cat's a good cat mom," the vet tech smiled. She'd known me for a long time, as had the vet.

When my mind was in a calmer state, I wondered how vets and their personnel handled customers like me. Are we scary? Do they get special training for us? The vet and the staff need to navigate all sorts of stuff—the illnesses of animals and various anatomical systems, the emotions of the owners, downright cruelty in some cases, heartbreaking scenarios of many kinds. I could not do it.

Doesn't everyone fall apart when their animal is ill? We all fall apart differently. I would have camped out at the vet's office if I had to—put a sleeping bag on the floor and spent every last moment with Jamie Tuega.

It's my personal blessing and a curse. I've never been the kind of person that can matter-of-factly say, "It's time, put him down." I admire people with this directness. They are decisive and their emotions don't wreck their lives. But I'm guessing. How can I really know how grief affects each person?

The vet and the tech gently took my orange cat away from me. In a calm and compassionate way, the vet told me to come back in one hour. I drove away shaking, hands on the old Tacoma steering wheel. Off somewhere to kill this time in a coffee shop alone. I was not fit for company.

I PULLED UP TO THE VET's office at the appointed hour, a sick feeling in my stomach. The vet came out of the building to my car, and he was smiling. Something dropped away and I felt as if a hundred rivers of stress were streaming nonstop from my neck, down my shoulders, down my arms, out my fingers.

I TOOK JAMIE HOME. We were not out of the woods yet, but there was still some hope. High stakes medical issues always have so many unknowns.

"Give it a couple days," the vet said. There were antibiotics to give. If it was a cut, and not a tumor, it would go away in a few days, and Jamie would be able to eat again.

I was encouraged when we get home. We offered Jamie some raw turkey burger and he was very interested. He grabbed at it with jaws and teeth, even though he couldn't use his tongue. It was to be one of the many peaks and valleys in the coming months of this journey with Jamie.

Beans Don't Wait, Basil Doesn't Wait, Cats Don't Wait

I'm under a lot of deadlines lately. I'm racing to get the vegetables from the garden picked, inside, and taken care of (i.e., processed, canned, frozen, stored) before we get our first killing frost. This is actually good for me, because I'm the sort of person who needs a deadline. I get very productive when there are consequences if I don't act.

There can be consequences if I don't act on behalf of my cats. I have become better about taking action quickly over the years, even though I may dread what I find out. Getting more fearless, and remembering that ultimately, I have my cats' interests in mind, are good goals. When I took Jamie to the vet on Monday, I was nervous, a little scared, and stressed. A cat not eating brings back other memories of other loved cats who had stopped eating, and ultimately passed on. But as badly as I didn't want to go to the vet, the urge for definitive answers drove me there. We don't know everything yet, and I have no idea what Jamie's life path looks like in the future. I do know that his organ functions are great for a cat his age, and that makes me happy.

More than anything, this is an exercise in staying present. I only have now. Cherish, observe, take part in Now. The past is gone, and the future isn't here yet. Love my cats in the moment, and thank them for their lessons.

Cleo—Beginning to Drive

MY JOURNEY WITH CATS didn't start until well into adulthood. As a child, I'd been much more interested in dogs. I learned about all the canine breeds and made special walking detours on my way home from grade school to visit favorite dogs. One tiny white poodle named Champagne jumped joyously up on her fence in the back yard so I could pet her. The pet owners humored me and smiled when I stopped by. I continue this habit to this day, regularly visiting two sweet Corgis in my town's Dollar Barn store. The owner humors me.

As a child, I fed my love of dogs and read every Albert Payson Terhune book I could get my hands on. Terhune wrote books about the collies he bred and their heroic endeavors—imagine *Lassie Come Home* with a lot more detail about the dog world and a bigger cast of characters. Imagine expert glimpses into the dog-show world, and wonderful representations of the souls and psyches of Terhune's collies, set in the countryside of New Jersey. My imagination ran rampant.

In my thirties, thanks to a girlfriend who was a true cat lover, I discovered cats. I spent time with her cats (two gray and black tabbies) and slowly, these cats grew on me. I began to appreciate a cat's quiet way. Yet these two cats also made me laugh. I remember having breakfast at my friend's house and one of the cats draping himself around my shoulders as I ate. The cat tried sneakily to intersect the fork that traveled from my plate to my mouth. I spent more and more time with these cats, and I began volunteering at Humane Societies in St. Paul and Minneapolis, just to walk the dogs and pet and brush the cats.

Later in my thirties, I broke up with a nice person who could not lick his alcoholism. We'd lived together in a well taken care of basement apartment in a cute neighborhood, right near the Mississippi River in St. Paul.

Making the decision to break up (my decision, not his) released me of a burden of living with an alcoholic on the edge, a big burden I hadn't realized I'd been carrying. Newfound energy surged through me. I told the boyfriend to leave our apartment and I dragged his furniture into the apartment hallway. I phoned him and told him his dresser was outside the apartment.

"What if someone takes it?" he pleaded.

"Come and get it faster." I didn't care if he thought I was mean. I didn't care if someone else took the furniture. The weeks stretched in front of me, exciting and full of promise. Suddenly I was free—free from his lies and his covering up about drinking, free from worrying about him, free to live my life the way I wanted, free from the stupid complications of alcohol—something that had never been particularly special to me.

To celebrate this turning point in my life, I did two things I'd wanted to do for a long time. First, I bought myself a small tent. Camping in the wilderness is something I've loved since I was introduced to the Boundary Waters wilderness area as a teenager. I happily envisioned wilderness camping trips I would take, unimpaired either by a scared boyfriend (the alcoholic, who was afraid of the wilderness) or a couch potato (a former boyfriend who preferred to drive through northern Minnesota rather than camp or hike or paddle in it).

The second big decision I made was to adopt a cat.

My girlfriend's cats had convinced me a cat would make a great apartment companion. I knew a cat would be wonderful company and I knew there were lots of cats that needed homes. I eagerly anticipated picking out a cat. I couldn't wait to snuggle with a feline and make it part of my new family and my new life.

On a Saturday, I drove out to the Hennepin County Golden Valley shelter in search of a cat. I remember it was a bright spring day, and I may have stopped at Eloise Butler Wildflower Garden (part of Theodore Wirth Regional Park in Minneapolis) along the way to take a quick walk.

After parking at the shelter, I walked into the clean but noisy adoption area. A chorus of barking rose from the section of the shelter that housed the dogs—behind a visible interior door and containing rows of kennels with cement floors. Occasionally, between the barks of the dogs, one could hear the meow of a cat, perhaps trying to get the attention of passersby. There were several people wandering through the premises—Saturday was often the busiest day of the Humane Society's week.

I was pretty sure I wanted an adult cat, not a kitten. Kittens are adorable and come with their own charm. I'd come to love my friend's adult cats with their fully formed personalities. Adult cats seem to have stories to tell if we know how to listen. Also, adult cats have a harder time getting adopted. I knew this from my experience as an off-and-on shelter volunteer at the St. Paul Humane Society.

"Mrowww."

I turned and saw a cage in the center of the cat adoption area. The "mrowww" was offered clearly, with authority. The voice had a slight nasal twang, and undeniable confidence. A gray cat stared directly at me and held a paw out through the slats of the stainless steel cage door. Her eyes were green. I walked closer and touched her paw. She grabbed on lightly with her claws, not hurting, but intentionally letting me know she wanted contact.

Looking behind her, I noticed a long-haired white cat with brilliant blue eyes and peach tones huddled back in the corner. The white cat had an air of depression or despair. I could not get her to engage with me.

The gray cat continued to converse with me and grab me with her paw. I noticed all her paws were white. The white cat stayed in the corner and didn't make a sound.

A quick glance at the written description the shelter provided (on a pink index card taped to the cage) identified the cats as young spayed females. These cats had been given up when their older owner went into a nursing home. The owner had requested they be adopted together, as they were buddies and as it would put the owner's mind at ease. The gray cat was named Cleo. The white cat, Tigger.

Two cats?

I'd not considered it.

Taking a breath, I studied them more closely. The white cat regarded me from afar. The gray cat schmoozed, talked, and wagged her paw through the cage slats. When I opened the cage to pick up the gray cat, she put her paws around my neck and hugged me.

Two cats? Why not?

I knew my apartment would allow up to two pets. Not sure about the white cat, but smitten with the gray one, I took them both home.

The white cat, Tigger, spent a lot of time hiding and being quiet. She was obviously upset with the changes in her life and I hoped she would adjust, given time. I gave her as much love as I could and tried to give her the space she seemed to need. She and Cleo snuggled together whenever possible and I was glad for this one constant in Tigger's life.

Cleo become a real clown.

You know your cats are delighted you're home from traveling when . . .

. . . They ALL pile on the bed at once and guard you with jealous glances.

. . . They start acting up, showing off, play fighting, and howling, and your partner says, "They didn't do any of this while you were gone."

. . . They ride your shoulders and refuse to get down.

. . . They instantly revert to your schedule of feeding them, even if your partner or roommate fed them on a completely different schedule.

. . . They do those cute things reserved for when you are there. For example, Chester only comes on the bed when I get in, but he lies on my husband's chest to look at me.

. . . They make an extra effort to drag the toys out of the corner. Balls are batted, a catnip pillow toy is smacked across the floor like a soccer ball, or a floor-length curtain becomes a soft barrier for two cats to bat at each other while they roll around on the rug.

. . . They purr in unison, loudly and all night long. You hear them since sleep is impossible with two people and five cats on a full-sized bed.

She happily chattered in the windowsill at birds, she hugged me regularly, and she stole chicken from kitchen countertops. Life after the alcoholic boyfriend was proving fun. One time when I was standing over the kitchen table, slicing meat, Cleo vertically jumped up between me and the table, snatched the meat, landed back on the floor, and ran off with a smug look on her face. Cleo made her misbehaviors all better with those paw hugs around my neck. I grew attached to her in a very short time.

"I'm so happy!" I told them both. Cleo hugged me around the neck as I held her. Tigger was at least starting to respond to my petting. I hoped she could come out of herself.

A few weeks after I adopted the cats, Cleo suddenly went into convulsions and vomited bile on the living room floor. I felt my throat close up in panic. "Cleo!" I cried.

UNEXPECTED PET EMERGENCIES never get easier, but this first one was particularly traumatic. By all appearances, Cleo was a young and healthy cat with a long life ahead of her. She'd had her physical, and was up-to-date on her shots.

I rushed her to the Humane Society, where she was still within the timeframe for a checkup. They kept her for observation, but called me the next day.

"Kitty is really ill and has chronic pancreatitis," the vet said. "I recommend you let us put her to sleep." He explained it was congenital, and not curable.

I don't remember exactly what went through my mind. I don't remember how quickly I consented or if I hesitated. I am sure I must have felt empty, as if space opened up before me, a void created by the fact that Cleo was leaving, quickly and abruptly. I don't know whether it sank in that I would never see my gray cat with the white paws again. I would never feel those paws hugging me around the neck.

"Yes," I said. My first encounter with cat loss. The grief would hit me later.

And grieve I did. I cried with a force that surprised me. I called a woman friend from Al-Anon. My friend suggested my grief was coming out sideways from leaving the boyfriend. But it didn't feel that way. The cat who had reached out to me was gone. Who would hug me with little white paws again? Who would snuggle her little round gray head under my chin, and make me laugh? It seemed cruel to get such a gift and have it snatched away.

I grew up with tough love. I am well aware that things could be a lot worse, and that many suffer more than I can imagine. But it hurt.

I hope Cleo wasn't scared. I hope she had a good life with me, even though her time with me was so short. I wish now that I had driven out to see her before they put her down. Why didn't I think of this option?

Animal communicators (some call them animal psychics) say our loved animals are much more matter-of-fact about death than we humans are. The animals know it's just a transition from one reality to another. I wonder if we humans are at a disadvantage with our emotions and our egos. I'd sure like to be more matter-of-fact about death, and life.

Cleo was the first cat I bonded with as an adult. Many more cats would follow as I drove through life; driving with cats to the vet, driving to surgery, walking through the days loving cats and their unique ways. Cat lovers understand; dog lovers understand; anyone with an animal companion understands.

In retrospect I think Cleo's gift was to pair me up with Tigger. Tigger eventually blossomed and became a powerful teacher in her own right.

Nicknames

I'm a word person, so some of my cats' nicknames, and the process of their evolution, really amuse me. How does "Jamie" turn into "Jamie-tuega" (pronounced "too-ga")? And what does "Tuega" mean? And what does Jamie think when I start singing "Tuega-Tuega-Tuega" to him?

Yeah . . . we're all crazy here.

Sometimes I bet the cats are smiling inside, thinking, "Glad I can amuse you and bring you so much happiness." Because they do. Every time I use one of these silly nicknames, I smile. They probably wouldn't mean a thing to anyone else. Do people do the same thing with kids? I bet they do.

Here's another one—Kieran is "pretty boy." Why? Just because he is a very pretty, unusual-looking boy. I don't use his nickname a lot, though. Recently, we have started to call him "Quinoa," maybe because it sounds a little like Kieran, or at least has a "K" sound at its beginning.

Kali actually started out as "Misty." But a friend of mine pointed out that this cat did not have the personality of a Misty, and was more like the fierce Hindu goddess Kali. "Kali" stuck. Sometimes we call her "Growler" because she used to growl a lot.

Rama (black cat) probably has some of the silliest nicknames. I love the name Rama, but we quickly started calling him Rama Dassa (after Ram Dass). That got turned into Dassa Dude. And somehow, it all became "Dyson." Not necessarily after the vacuum cleaner, though Dyson/Rama does eat like a horse, or a vacuum. We call him Dyson all the time.

It makes me wonder if nicknames influence behavior, or vice versa . . .

Tips for Driving with Cats

Today I had to make another trip to the vet—this time for Karma, who has a cold. Karma's eye was red and she was holding it slightly shut. This set off alarm bells for me since Jamie had an eye ulcer earlier this year, and ended up losing an eye. So even though nothing looked awry, I took the time to get Karma in and I'm glad I did.

The vet put stain on Karma's eye to check for ulcers (there were none). Eyes can get inflamed and red just from these colds, but the vet understood why I was a little gun-shy. Karma was a tiny bit dehydrated—sometimes congested cats don't feel like drinking—so the vet gave Karma some subcutaneous fluid. The vet called it a "backpack" since it's given via needle over the shoulders and upper spine.

Having made many of these trips to my vet, I've learned to plan for as smooth a trip as possible. Here's what I include:
· A cat carrier. This is safest for the cat, and you. Even if you have a cat who sits nicely while you drive, put them in a carrier for safety in case of an accident, or to contain them.
· Plenty of rags, especially if you have a cat who gets carsick. Paper towels work, too.
· A disposable bag for soiled rags or paper towels.
· A container with soapy water. (I admit, I've never thought of this. After today, though, I was wishing I'd had this in the car to clean out the carrier so Karma could've had a nicer ride after she got sick.)
· An extra carrier, if you don't want to deal with cleaning a messy carrier. If the cat gets sick, clean her to the best of your ability, and put her in the second carrier.
· A cell phone in case you break down, especially if you drive in remote country like some of us do. It also helps to know where reception is or isn't good along your route.
· Built-in time for your trip, in case you need to pull over and take care of your cat if she does get carsick, or for some other reason. Plan ahead.
· Food and water for longer road trips.
· Any required current vaccination information (if you're crossing into another country where this might be required).
· Preps for weather. I try not to do routine vet stuff in the wintertime, just because I don't like traveling with animals when it is extremely cold out. I would be concerned for the animal if the car broke down in below-zero weather, for example. Of course, cold weather drivers usually have weather survival kits in their cars. If you're going to travel with your animals in the winter, make sure they also have a way to stay warm if your car breaks down.
· Similarly, I try not to schedule routine vet stuff in the high heat of the summer, if there is a chance my cat might have to wait in the car anywhere on that particular trip. A few seconds in a too-hot car can be fatal to dogs, cats, and other animals, even if the windows are cracked open.

Tigger—Running in Circles

IN 2012, I WAS VISITING relatives in Pittsburgh, Pennsylvania. The household I was staying in had a long-haired calico cat named Sammy. Sammy (a female) reminded of my cat Tigger—they were both beautiful in a coy and quiet way; both took their time to warm to new people but loved unreservedly once the bond was established. I loved Sammy, and I loved that she reminded me of Tigger. It was like having a bit of home with me when I was on the road, even though Tigger had been gone for many years.

If Cleo was the first cat I bonded with as an adult, then Tigger was the first cat I deeply bonded with and had the privilege of being with for many years.

After Cleo died, Tigger slowly began to come out of her shell. It took several months and I was gentle with her as I learned to live with cats and began to understand them. I let her take her time. We were mimicking each other, I think—tentatively exploring a new direction in life for each of us.

I found myself enjoying life free from the drama of another's alcoholism. I had no one to take care of except Tigger, and I poured myself into observing her and learning as much about cats as I could.

There's a photo I have of my mother sitting on a makeshift couch of mine, petting Tigger. Mom is smiling and Tigger is relaxed, stretched out on her side and easily giving my mother her belly—a true sign of cat trust. In the photo, Tigger's beauty is apparent. She has cream-colored fur and a pretty peach-colored spot on her rear leg. Her ice blue eyes are stunning. To this day, I can't believe I didn't notice her beauty at the Humane Society. I was so taken with Cleo. Attitude really does create beauty, and Tigger was beginning to come into her own.

Tigger had turned the corner and started to trust and enjoy life with me. Our days were pleasant and wonderful—I was enjoying peaceful singleness and contemplating graduate school in forestry. Tigger had started to put on weight and began to shed the lethargy of depression, showing the energy of a healthy young cat. She began to do cat things like sitting in the window, chattering at birds, head butting me, and playing with the new toys I bought for her.

Tigger had no idea she'd be moving to a few different households with me before we settled down. I knew by now that cats can be place-sensitive, but Tigger would navigate some of the transitions better than I did.

The first transition involved leaving my pretty, well-kept apartment near the Mississippi River. The apartment that I'd kicked the alcoholic boyfriend out of had clean-looking black and white tiles on the kitchen floor, varnished woodwork, and a classic old St. Paul ambiance. I had not planned to leave this apartment but to my dismay, my ex-boyfriend took a caretaker position in the building and would be living right down the hall. He had told our good landlords nothing about our breakup.

The landlords were pretty surprised when they found out about the breakup from me and realized I wanted to move from the building. I tried to tough it out and stay at the apartment, but after a few weeks, I knew I didn't want to be there, walking past the ex's apartment near the front door and feeling he knew what I was up to. I needed to put symbolic and real space between us.

Tigger and I moved to a junky apartment in a scary part of town, just a few miles from the nice apartment by the river. I can't imagine living in such a place now but at the time, it seemed perfectly normal. I feel fortunate I've never had to live in such a place since. Roaches roamed the kitchen and never went away, regardless of how many roach motels I bought or how hard I washed the floors and the walls. Loud parties on the floor below kept me up at night until 3:00 a.m. It seemed I could never get the apartment clean enough. There was always a layer of grime, grease, smell, or oldness that just couldn't be washed away.

I had hardly any furniture to fill this fairly big apartment, which included a big living room, two bedrooms, a dining room, sizable kitchen, and bathroom. I have a memory of Tigger lying calmly in one empty room, watching me, as if she was waiting for me to come to my senses. She stayed her happy self and continued to thrive, even though the apartment had a distinctly depressing aura.

Tigger was bonding with me, and I had the feeling she'd be happy to live wherever I went. I also had the solace of my piano, which had been moved (by professional piano movers) up a scary-looking and decrepit rear stairwell on the backside of the apartment building. The movers were sure everything was going to collapse on them, as they somehow got the piano up three stories. When they finished the job, I knew they couldn't be paid enough to do such a job again.

True to my past patterns, single life would not last long for me. At least my choices in men were getting better. I dated a professor who was very interested in me, and quite outdoorsy. Tigger liked him and he liked cats. The first time he held her, he cradled her in his arms, belly up. She seemed to be tolerating it, but I thought I saw the beginning of a gleam in her blue eyes.

"Careful," I warned him. "She bites."

"I bite back," he laughed. And that was the fun and interesting thing about this man. He had a gentle exterior and a backbone, too. We had a few enjoyable dates together, but the chemistry was not there for me, and I was simply not ready for this man. Perhaps all was meant to be, since ceasing dating this man led to the next relationship—meeting Chris, the man I would marry.

I FIRST NOTICED CHRIS when we both were enrolled as graduate students in the College of Natural Resources at the University. As paid graduate assistants, we had our own research to do, but we were also at the disposal of our hiring professors. Thus, we had offices (shared with several other grads) and the use of a computer lab. Graduate assistants did anything from assisting with teaching, helping write peer-reviewed publications for professors, or helping the college run

Tips for the Caregiver

I'll share what I've learned during intense care-giving for my animal companions. A lot of this is good common sense, but it never hurts to be reminded.

Being the caregiver to your animals (or your people) can be an intense, demanding, and emotionally draining job. To take care of yourself when you're a caregiver:

· Attend to your health. Exercise, get outside and walk, eat good foods. Even if you only have time for a five-minute walk, run, or stretch, it will help your mental state. Drink plenty of water.

· Sleep. Your body will tell you when it must rest. Listen to it.

· Breathe. Yoga uses a deep diaphragmatic breath (inhale through the nose, exhale through the nose). Close your eyes and breathe for one, two, or five minutes. Let yourself go. You'll be amazed at what this little effort will give you in the form of relaxation.

· Get out of the situation for a while if possible. If someone can take over for a few hours or a day, get out of the house, away from the animals or person. Take in different scenery. Let yourself think about something else. Release any worry. Do something good for yourself—a beautiful walk around a lake, a good cup of coffee, a massage, a heart-to-heart with a trusted friend—whatever works in your situation.

· "Reframe instead of blame." We second guess ourselves during times of crisis. Mind chatter such as "I didn't catch this in time . . ." "I should have done this, this or this," "I should have gone to a different vet," etc. is not necessarily helpful or productive. We do the best we can with what we have.

· Being a caregiver for an animal companion is a high calling, in my opinion, so I think it makes good sense to honor yourself with good self care, when needed.

symposia or conferences for resource professionals.

Chris and I both spent a lot of time in the College's tiny computer lab for graduate students. The lab had the nicest machines (IBM PCs) in the college. Graduate students with research or teaching assistance-ships usually had ancient and bulky Commodore computers in their offices, hand-me-downs from faculty and staff. If you needed to use a nice machine or print something decent, you used the computer lab.

Chris seemed to be in the lab at all hours of the night. He was a doctoral student in the College's water quality program and he worked very hard. Coming from a long line of workaholics on my mother's side, I took notice and probably approved. (It was a value that had been driven into me, and in a strange way, it was familiar and comforting). Chris seemed shy but also seemed increasingly warm and friendly to me. When he asked me out, I remember being completely surprised. I blurted out, "Yes," in a state of shock. Chris said okay and took off quickly, probably just as shocked as I was.

I checked Chris out with a few mutual grad student friends.

"Wendy," I asked one of our friends-in-common. "What's he like? Is he dangerous? Safe to go on a date with?"

Wendy got a slow smile on her face, which started small and got bigger. She looked as if something she'd never pictured had suddenly entered her world.

"Hmmmm," she said. "Hmmmm." Wendy was in Chris's program and had a partner and kids of her own. "Yeah. He's nice. Very nice." She assured me Chris was a decent person and in her opinion, safe on a first date. "I can see this . . ." she murmured. I had no idea what "this" would turn into.

ASSURED CHRIS WAS SAFE, we had our first date—a North Stars/Bruins hockey game in a suburb of Minneapolis. On a bitterly cold night at the stadium after the game, Chris's old Subaru conked out and wouldn't start. We rode home with the car on a hook, sitting together in the front of a tow truck. Chris was embarrassed at this unexpected ending to an otherwise fine date. I laughed and told him not to worry. We had a great time—even though I didn't understand hockey and still don't—and we continued to date.

Not long after, I took Chris up to northern Wisconsin for cross-country skiing in the Chequamegon National Forest. Things progressed quickly. We danced in the kitchen of the condo we stayed in. I was happy to feel how well we fit together. Chris was only four inches taller than I was, and we both had an innate and good sense of rhythm and love of music. (Later I would find out that Chris was an excellent drummer and guitarist.) We started seeing each other often.

Some people are naturally good at service and generosity, and I admire these people. There's a cliché I don't remember the exact words to, that states your real friends are the ones who show up when you need help moving. Chris has a generous heart to this day. He helped me move out of the junky apartment with roaches, and I felt instant relief upon leaving the place. Until the very moment of moving out, I hadn't realized my being there felt so wrong and asynchronous. Sometimes, I guess I need to leave a situation to see it more clearly.

Driving with Cats

I moved into an apartment in South St. Paul by myself. Chris and I weren't ready to try living together yet. The two-story South St. Paul building was older and not fancy, but I knew the landlord—a friend of mine from Al-Anon—and I knew he was honest. In some ways, the location was dicey. The apartment building was across the street from a lively bar. One morning at 2:00 a.m. I woke up abruptly—my sleep shattered by the broken glass of a car windshield; vestiges of a bar fight. But I never felt unsafe in this apartment, and it didn't have the icky and strange energy of the previous place.

Why Care About Cats?

None of my friends have ever asked me, "Why do you care about cats?" to my face. They know they'd get a pretty incredulous look from me, or maybe a passionate diatribe. A true friend appreciates me for who I am.

It is a good ethical question, though. Why care about animals? Why take care of cats? Aren't there a billion other world problems that need addressing? Are the needs of people more important? Are the needs of stray or suffering animals any greater than that of suffering people or our taxed planet?

I don't have a definitive answer. I don't think there is a definitive answer. But here's what I think.

We all comprise the planet—people, animals, nature . . . all of it. How we treat people or animals or anything or ourselves is a reflection on how we treat the planet—because we are all the planet.

We may have a calling, if we are wise enough to recognize it. Following your calling is a wonderful way to live life and achieve something great in the finite time we have here. Finding your calling is a joyous thing. Your calling may be raising and nurturing children. You may be an activist for peace. You may fight to end poverty. You may create beautiful quilts. You may love nature.

I have a calling to write. I have a calling to care about cats. I have a calling to do yoga, to teach yoga, and to connect with people on a deep level. To me, a calling seems to be intrinsic—a part of our "wiring" we couldn't change if we tried. (I'm talking about true callings here—not a "calling" someone else tries to impose on you, or a "calling" you try to wear that doesn't really fit.)

This doesn't mean I care any less about the myriad of other causes. It just means I'm channeling my energy where there's the most passion for me. I'm acting in sync with my wiring. I care about cats and I will continue to care about them. I will take care of my cats to the best of my ability and I will support organizations that do amazing work for the welfare of animals.

Finding a calling is a wonderful thing. The world, the planet, WE, all benefit when we act in sync with our values, our wiring, and our own deepest truth.

Chris stayed over often, making the fifteen-minute drive in his Subaru and parking on the street. The apartment had an old linoleum floor in the kitchen that would probably be called retro, if it hadn't been the real thing. The pattern on the floor was a beige, blue, and red funky paisley. Chris and I loved to pull aside the one piece of furniture in the kitchen—the table—and clear the big floor for dancing. We'd polka or two-step to Cajun music, something we do today in our kitchen in our log house in northern Minnesota.

Tigger seemed much more at home in the South St. Paul apartment than she had in the roach-infested predecessor—she'd watch us dance in the kitchen from her spot in the adjacent living room. She liked to snuggle up on an old pea-green couch that a friend had given me. I still have a picture of her on that couch. The South St. Paul apartment will always have strong memories for me of Tigger and Chris and our bonding.

Chris invented a game with Tigger. We often ordered pizza delivery. Tigger loved the smell of a freshly delivered pizza—the aroma of soft crust, the tomato sauce, the sizzle of greasy melting cheese. In the way cats do, she'd jump on our thrift store dining room table, acting coy and quiet as if she couldn't be seen—even though she was right in our vision.

Chris would take on the voice of Tigger, high and dainty.

"You can't see me," he'd say, pretending he was speaking for Tigger.

She would creep up closer, paw at the ready, eyes honed in on the tip of a triangular piece of pizza.

"Just one padded paw . . ." Chris would whisper .

I laughed, loving the silly cat games, loving a guy that would play these cat games and seemed to enjoy them.

"Just one padded paw!"

We'd cut off a tiny piece from the tip of the pizza, a symbol of the game, and give it to Tigger, who would snap it up.

We made a story, a tradition we would continue through a long line of cats; a practice I bet many cat or dog or pet lovers take on in the secrecy of their homes. We made a cute story up where Tigger would sneak up to the pizza, swat it onto the floor, and proudly carry it off into another room like a freshly caught mouse. We always cut off the tiny tips at the end of a pizza slice and let her eat them. I loved that Chris indulged me in these silly games and seemed to enjoy them. I loved that Tigger and he had a strong bond. Tigger obviously approved of Chris. We were together quite a bit, Chris and I during the day at school, and Chris and Tigger and I at night.

AFTER ONE MORE APARTMENT, and then my first small house, Chris and I got married in 1994. (Two more cats had joined the household.) Marriage was a smooth transition, as Chris and I had been living together in the house for two years. Our wedding was moderate in size—150-200 people and a reception that featured a folk dancing band. A friend of mine snapped pictures of me in my wedding dress holding each of the three cats we had at the time—Tigger, Jamie, and Milo. I posed on the front stoop of our house, holding one cat for each picture.

In our new household with three cats, Tigger was definitely the low cat on the totem pole. Her sweet but nervous personality didn't stand up to persnickety Jamie or streetsmart Milo. Milo, a big orange tom, mercilessly chased Tigger onto the tops of the furnace ducts in the basement. The ducts were attached to the basement ceiling and neither Jamie nor Milo were small enough to follow Tigger into those narrow spaces. However, they made sure she hid for a while. Or perhaps it was her own decision. A highly sweet and sensitive nature was the essence of Tigger. A good friend of ours said Tigger reminded him of me. I took it as a compliment.

NINE OR TEN YEARS LATER, Chris and I had moved to northern Minnesota for his job. A slow and subtle change started to surface in Tigger. Cats bear careful watching, as they tend to hide their illnesses. Something can be very very wrong with a cat before it's obvious to the humans around that cat.

After twenty years of caring for cats and helping them through illnesses and the end of life, I have learned to be very attuned to any change in behavior. Even a change in the way they sit or lie down can mean that something is up. As Tigger was my first cat, I was about to get some interesting lessons.

At that time, my freelance office was in the house. I worked at the kitchen table, writing articles and editing for clients, largely online. Tigger began pacing around the table. She'd walk as I worked, endlessly circling the perimeter of the table. I knew something was up but I had no idea what it might be.

Then Tigger started pooping outside her litter box.

This is a sure sign that something is not right. Some vets believe the cat is trying to get your attention. Some believe that physiological changes cause this behavior. Perhaps it is a mixture of both. I tried to put myself in her place and understand the confusion she might be feeling. I told her all would be okay, and I would try to understand what was going on and not give up on her.

Reasoning that a dog won't dirty its quarters (usually, a kennel), I put Tigger in the bathroom for two weeks with her litter box. The bathroom is small. I figured if she had limited options for spaces to poop in, she might get the idea. I visited her all the time and reassured her that all would be fine. Something worked, and she began using the box again.

Unfortunately, a lump showed up on Tigger's rear leg in the vicinity of a vaccine site. In the 1990s, vets were just beginning to realize the feline leukemia vaccine (and other vaccines) can be associated with the formation of cancerous sarcomas. Sarcomas are aggressive cancer tumors that are hard to eradicate and keep growing back. Additionally, vets in my rural part of Minnesota, where cats are not often vaccinated for feline leukemia (because it has a low rate of occurrence), were not familiar with seeing sarcomas present as a result of a vaccine.

How could my beautiful cat have such an ugly thing as cancer? I had the lump cut out but it returned quickly and more aggressively. I traveled the four hours to the cities to take Tigger to the University of Minnesota Veterinary Hospital. They recommended amputation of the rear leg to try and cease the spread of the aggressive cancer. Horrified, and wanting to save her, I agreed.

I stayed with her at the hospital as much as I was able. Staff seemed surprised at my determination to hang around.

"You're dedicated," one of the veterinary staff said to me. I remember sitting on a smooth tile floor, in a room full of stainless steel cages, my arm half in and half out of Tigger's cage. I could have spent the night there, I was so tired.

I nodded, numb with exhaustion and emotion. Grief always kicks my butt—worse than the most physical work on our land, worse than the hardest workout. Grief beats it all.

Cats are more than cats to me. They are not people, but as a memorable quote suggests, they are something we can't even come close to understanding. Therefore, my bond with cats is complicated. I will go to lengths that many probably wouldn't take. We are not rich, and we might be a lot richer if I didn't seek out major medical care for my cats.

Tigger came through her surgery. Animals are very adaptable. They get around quite well on three legs if needed. However, this was very new to me. Tigger had a huge incision and seemed very angry about losing the leg. I felt terrible. Eventually, she adapted.

Sometime later, I have a memory of an incident with our stepladder, which I had dragged into the house to wash the walls and the ceilings. The stepladder was old and paint-spattered—a hand-me-down from Chris's dad who was a house painter. With her three legs, Tigger climbed that ladder, all white/peachy soft fur and blue eyes. Tigger was proud of herself. I could see it in the satisfied expression in her face and I could feel it in her confident body movement.

Sadly, it turned out that the cancer had spread into Tigger's lungs. We had not been able to get it by taking the leg. My gentle and sensitive cat was in real trouble.

Tigger had very little time left and she made it clear she wanted me near her. I spent every moment I could with her. These times—and

I have been through many, since—are always loaded. My heart was breaking open. I had love and endless patience for her, but often had little reserves for anything else. I walked in a local walk (the Sand Lake Shuffle) to raise money for cancer. At the same time, exhausted with grief, I railed inside. Why couldn't I walk to raise money for Tigger? (I suppose I could have, but I wasn't being very rational at the time.) Sometimes people had remission from this horrible illness. Why couldn't Tigger have remission? Why couldn't the cancer go away, for good? I hoped against hope for a miracle. I think we all do this.

It is the strangest mental place, and I have occupied it many times since. I'll call it the Hospice Time, for lack of a better term. A beloved animal companion is at the end of their life. The brain is simultaneously in two places—on the one hand, heavy sorrow hangs over the house. We all know what's coming even though we don't want to admit it. What we don't know, is how it will come. We know NOTHING. It is a huge slap in the face about our inability to be in control.

Unconditional Love

From my cats, I've learned I am capable of unconditional love.

Certainly, our animal companions give us unconditional love. We know this; we become used to it; we take it for granted.

But for me to realize I was capable of unconditional love was a revelation.

When I faced animal companion illness and inevitable death for the first time, it felt as if I was falling into an uncharted void. All of existence ripped open in front of me. That's as close as I can come to describing it. The deep grief of what I faced put me in a strange new place. Uncharted territory, indeed.

Tigger, the first cat who shared ten years with me, was diagnosed with cancer. After the initial shock and grief—how could my beautiful cat have horrible, ugly cancer?—I threw myself into service.

Perhaps this is something parents will relate to. I have no children and this was a first. I would do, and did do, everything I could for Tigger. And I did it with purity and without expectation—and without trying. I simply gave and gave. Unconditionally.

I monitored her constantly. Took charge of meds and food. Put her comfort above all else. Waited for a sign, if there was to be one, that the time had come if she needed assistance. Lost sleep. Cried. Loved. Laughed. Treasured every moment. Stroked her beautiful fur, seared her face and eyes and personality into my memory.

Death is a twisty path. We don't know how it will play out and we don't know what's around the corner. We don't know how it will end. All we can say for sure is that it will eventually come.

But never in my life have I felt as spiritual as when I gave this service to my cat. I would have done anything for her. And I realized as I was going through this, I had never been in this place before—the place of unconditional love. Giving without restraint. Giving without expectation or attachment to outcome.

May I always be open to the rich lessons my animal companions have for me.

On the other hand, we maintain an almost silly (foolish?) optimism. Maybe what we're doing will help. Maybe the cat or dog will take a turn for the better. You never know. It's optimism juxtaposed with deep despair; it's will and drive pitted against exhaustion and lack of control. I have never been through anything like it. As Tigger neared the end of her life, I never dreamed of how many times I'd go through this process again and again. Each time would be different, bringing its lessons, heartaches, love, and ongoing amazement at the incredible bond between us and our animal companions.

It seems my animals pass the way they want to. Tigger, the first to pass at home, led this trend. On a Friday, Tigger was not eating, and barely eliminating. She was still moving around, and keeping me in her sights. I called the vet with a heavy dread in my throat, and I'm sure I cried. I made a euthanasia appointment for Monday. As I've wondered many times since, I remember wondering how vet staff and veterinarians deal with the strength of other people's emotions. I know I couldn't work in a vet's office.

Through the weekend, I spent every moment I could with Tigger. She would cry out for me if I got too far away, even though she could follow me. I put her on the bed at night and Chris generously took the couch in the living room. I had no idea what was coming, or what to expect. I think this is what unnerves me most about the passing process—it's simply such an unknown. And I still struggle with the mystery. How can something so strong be broken? Why does death come? How can something so alive be gone, with such finality? These questions have not changed for me, and are just as strong now as they were years ago, as Tigger neared the end of her life.

The night before she passed, Tigger got wobbly and had a hard time standing up. Her eyes became dilated. I took her onto the bed with padding underneath her for any accidents, though she was eliminating very little. I slept next to her, with my hand on her all night.

She woke me at 5:00 a.m., or maybe I woke. Death is a strange time for me and I have come to discover, through many animal and people deaths, that different information opens up to me at this time.

Perhaps I am too tired to get in my way. Perhaps I am sensing another reality not usually available to me.

Tigger began to gasp, and her body may have shuddered. I stroked her and talked to her, crying and naked, oblivious to myself. I thought of yelling for Chris, but I didn't want to leave her side, and irrationally, I thought my yelling might scare her.

She passed, leaving life as she had entered my life many years ago—gracefully, sensitively, quietly.

WE BURIED TIGGER in the back yard. Chris made a beautiful headstone from a piece of five-eighths-inch plywood. He cut the wood into a silhouette of a cat's head, with a front profile and with curling white fur around the cape of her neck. Across the surface of the wood he painted a blue sky background with dreamy white clouds. On this he painted, "Tigger, Master Teacher, 1989-1999. Come Back Soon."

Seeing Divinity in the Eyes of a Dog (or Cat)

I was walking with my brother and his dog, Diego, a collie/greyhound mix, on a lovely San Francisco day in early fall. San Francisco is a real dog town, and many people are out with their dogs at all hours. The dogs act as an icebreaker. People who don't know each other or would never talk to each other will easily approach each other and meet new dogs and compare dog stories or information. The dogs are acting as a unifier!

A man approached with two beautiful Keeshonds. (A Keeshond is a friendly dog breed that looks like a small gray Samoyed.) My husband and I had a Keeshond (named Chinook) who had passed away a year prior.

The dogs looked at me intently. I petted them and the man and my brother and I talked about the dogs.

I can't use language to explain it, because I am not sure that language can capture it. I saw our dog Chinook in the eyes of those dogs—and not just because they were the same breed. I saw her in their eyes. It was as if she was coming through, saying, "Hello! I was never gone!" It stopped me in my tracks in a joyful way.

Pay attention! These moments are all around us.

Jamie Comes to Our House

JAMIE CAME TO US as a kitten, so small you could hold him in the palm of your hand. Chris and I were in the first year of our relationship and still living separately, but spending a lot of time in my apartment near the university we both attended. My beautiful cream colored cat, Tigger, had been alone for one year since Cleo's death. I thought it might be nice for Tigger to have a new cat friend. We figured we'd introduce a kitten, as Tigger might not take well to an older cat.

I knew cats well enough to know that with an introduction, anything is possible. Still, I hoped. I had optimistic visions of Tigger finally getting to mother the kitten she'd never had. I could picture the two cats snuggled together, purring loudly and in unison, in my bright living room. Maybe the nearby trains that so unnerved Tigger now would be ignored if she had a kitten to take care of.

Chris and I trooped off to a nearby pet store, in a nondescript suburban mini-mall, to pick out a kitten. I cannot remember why we didn't go to the Humane Society—every other cat I've had has either been a shelter adoptee or a rescued stray. Perhaps I didn't want to be tempted by the overload of older cats needing homes. Or maybe it was still too soon after Cleo's death to want to go back to a Humane Society.

In the pet store, six tiny orange kittens frolicked behind glass. Most of them shied away when they saw us. One of them boldly, yet quietly, approached us and looked at us through the class—studying our hands, looking into our eyes, with expectation. His eyelids had a shock of white that outlined green, arresting eyes. He easily fit into the palm of my hand. We took him home.

I err on the conservative side when it comes to introducing cats. I will take three weeks, if needed, to keep them separate and let them slowly get to know each other under doors. I want it to work out. I'm sure we took our time in my small, one-bedroom apartment. We gave Jamie the bedroom, and let Tigger have the run of the rest of the place.

Jamie's quiet, focused, indomitable will showed itself early. The height of our full-sized bed was likely ten times the length of Jamie. But he was having none of sleeping on the floor. Lying in bed, we heard determined clawing and scrabbling. Jamie clawed his way up the side of the bed and took up residence on my pillow. There he purred, and the volume from such a tiny body didn't seem possible. The purr filled the room, a deep and promising rumble. He made it clear what he wanted—proximity to our heads, and a choice spot on the bed every night.

Proximity to our heads turned out to be a love of Jamie's in other ways—he quickly learned to ride shoulders and loved it, and he loved head butting. He'd head butt us with real force, and he especially loved rubbing against Chris's chin when Chris hadn't shaved for a day. These intense preferences of Jamie's stayed with him during his whole life.

The big day came—time to introduce the cats. We opened the door. "Time to get to know each other," I said brightly.

Tender, sweet Tigger came up to the kitten Jamie.

Let Your Cat Help You Stay in the Moment

There are a zillion self-help books for every malady and situation possible. Some of them address living in the moment—i.e., not worrying about the past or the future, but staying firmly in the "now." This is a challenge in our crazy western culture.

But never fear, if you share your life with an animal companion, you don't need to buy a self-help book. Your companions will teach you everything you need to know about living in the now.

Here are some of the many ways our cats work hard to get us closer to enlightenment. They have an unbeatable bag of tricks, including:

. . . a bracing "ma-WOW!" It's dinner time, and your cat wants your attention Now.

. . . a soft, but firm head butt. Your cat wants you to know she owns you, and she wants your attention Now.

. . . a gentle and firm paw on your lap. Your cat wants a pet, or lap space, Now.

. . . the jingle of a cat ball, dropped at your feet. Or the sound of cat toys falling on the floor as your cat paws open the cat toy-drawer. Your cat wants to play Now.

. . . the persistent tap of a paw on your head, drawing you from your sleep. Your cat wants you to wake up Now.

Aren't they great? Bypass the self-help section in the bookstore and buy your cat or dog a treat. Then say thank you. They work hard to help us become better!

Jamie turned on her.

He chased her in circles around the apartment, through the living room, kitchen, tiny entryway, living room—again and again. Tigger shrieked with dismay and outrage. It was clear who was boss. My warm fuzzy visions quickly faded. Jamie remained dominant until the introduction of Milo, who put Jamie in his place. What goes around, comes around.

A Day at the Cat Farm

Here's a glimpse of my day, cat chores and all. These occur in any order that makes the process most efficient. Seasonal details vary:

Get up between 5:00 and 7:00 a.m.

If it's winter (i.e., most of the year, in Minnesota), get woodstove fire going in house. Tend fire until it catches.

Clean cat boxes. Refill cat bowls with water.

Unlock the office and start the woodstove fire there. Clean Kieran's litter box. Refresh Kieran's water.

Feed Kieran.

Feed housecats, mixing in any medicines or supplements needed, or giving any pills needed. Feed Rama in bedroom, since Rama would eat everyone else's food if he could. Feed Jamie in bathroom, since he likes to eat slowly and I want him to get as much food as he needs.

Sweep floor. Make bed.

Vacuum every few days to keep up on firewood dust, cat hair, debris from wood. We have a Dyson vacuum, which I highly recommend for pet owners with carpet—it is the BEST.

Let the dog out of her kennel and check her water.

Let chickens outside into their outdoor coop area. Feed and water them. Check for eggs (and periodically repeat, all day).

Eat if I'm hungry.

Do yoga. Walk or work out (running, walking, workout DVD, or cross-country skiing, depending on weather).

Do freelance work. Check on fires. Pay attention to each cat. Play with Kieran. Throw Chester's "baba" (the "baba" is Chester's favorite toy—a small catnip-stuffed pillow he loves to carry around, and adores fetching and retrieving).

Drive into town to teach yoga. Fold in errands on the way if needed.

Garden, mow the lawn, split firewood, or do any number of homestead projects, depending upon the season and depending upon freelance business workload.

Work into the night if freelance deadlines loom. (The pros and cons of working from home are proximity, and proximity.)

Otherwise, spend the evenings in the summer being outside as much as possible. Spend the evenings in the winter cozying up by the fire—cats, partner, and a good book nearby.

That's where I'm headed now.

Moving with Cats

IN 1994, MY HUSBAND and I left the city and moved to remote northern Minnesota. This transition was a big deal in our lives. Chris had been offered, and accepted, a job in northern Minnesota as a water quality biologist, a position which exactly fit his background.

Chris started the job up north right after Christmas of 1994. He took the cats with him (Tigger, Jamie, and Milo). Our realtor in the cities had told us it would be easier to show the house if the cats were gone. I really missed Chris, and not having the cats with me made Chris's absence even harder.

Chris moved into a rented trailer home on Highway 53, the main thoroughfare from Duluth to the Canadian border. It seems a busy highway to me now, but then, it looked like the most desolate place in the world. Perceptions change. This is one thing I have learned over and over again moving from city to country. As I have become more spoiled and used to the quiet, the slightest bit of traffic seems too much. But back then, fresh out of the cities, this new home was the most remote, quiet, and desolate place one could have asked for.

I drove up with Chris to help him move in. Like many Twin Citians, I had been "up north," but only along the beautiful and touristy North Shore of Lake Superior. Never had I ventured straight north of Duluth to the Range and beyond. To my untrained city eyes, the landscape was sparse and scary. The whining of the cats in their carriers magnified my mood. I wondered what we were getting into. If rural living had occurred in my family history, it was likely centuries ago, and probably in agrarian Poland. My immediate family of origin was very urban. To say I was unprepared was an understatement.

I remember pulling into the driveway of the trailer home. There was an inch or two of snow on the ground and it was cold and crackly with air temps that were probably below zero. The driveway was short and dipped down quickly from the shoulder of the highway. I remember wondering whether it'd be hard to get out of the driveway and onto the road if the snow was slippery. The cats were restless after the four-hour drive and ready to be let out of their cages. I'd followed Chris all the way up—he'd driven our small Toyota truck and I was driving the Volkswagen Rabbit.

We got the cats inside first, and let them out of their cages to explore the trailer. They quickly found places to hide in the double wide, which had a living room, kitchen, small dining area, three bedrooms, a laundry room and a bath. They took a week or so to get used to the new place. By then, I was back in the cities at work, missing Chris and the cats terribly. However, I visited almost every weekend.

City Cat, Country Cat

Moving from the city to the country was one of the biggest transitions in my life. I learned a whole new way of being. My time is spent very differently than it was when I lived in the city. I sometimes feel as if I still have a foot in both worlds, or maybe I should phrase that differently. I have a foot both in a professional white-collar world (i.e., my work I do) and a farm world (the other work I do). Sometimes they tug at each other. Farm stuff needs to happen when it happens (i.e., plants need to be picked now, the garden needs to go in now). Work needs to be done now too. When both the nows happen at the same time, it gets interesting.

What did moving to the country mean for my cats?

They didn't go outside in the city and they don't go outside in the country. On the other hand, I have friends who have very savvy indoor/outdoor cats in the country. These cats have lived a long time because they seem very smart about not straying too far from the house. And they have accessible shelter from the weather when they need it. It's not a risk I've been willing to take with my cats, though a part of me wishes they could go outside and enjoy the wind and the smells.

My country cats probably catch more mice than they did in the city. My orange cat Milo had a special inauguration to the country not long after we landed here. He cornered a weasel in the trailer we were renting. Thankfully, neither Milo nor the weasel hurt each other and we were able to herd the weasel out of the house.

The veterinarian is farther away in the country, and the roads are icier in the winter—all things to think about in the daily care of cats. I try to be prepared as possible and have backup plans if I need to get a cat to the vet. And vets in the country are understanding of the distances that are a way of life up here. They'll mail medications to me; they'll consult on the phone if necessary. Life works differently in the country—it has to. It is shaped by the lay of the land and the distances and the elements and it affects us all—humans or our animal companions.

We racked up phone bills in the days before mobile technology. The separation was hard on us both and it would go on for five more months until I sold my house and closed in the cities. I don't remember my final drive out of the cities, but I'm sure I knew in my heart that a new type of life was about to begin and that I had passed a new milestone in my life.

Kieran and Chester, adopted after the big move.
(Photo courtesy of the author.)

Act II
Jamie—Driving into the Unknown

THREE DAYS PASSED after my twenty-year-old cat Jamie's visit to the vet. Jamie was not eating on his own. I wanted to hang on to my earlier optimism. Was I an optimist or simply a person in denial?

Chris and I began syringe-feeding Jamie canned food. This required work and time. The canned food had to have a really smooth consistency to get through the syringe. We watered it down and made it just thin enough to get it through the opening. We also started syringing Jamie water. I wasn't as comfortable with that, knowing he could aspirate fluid. But I didn't know what else to do, short of putting him down. And we couldn't put him down. In a few more days, he seemed to have strength back from the increased food and water he was taking in. Better yet, he seemed to still be enjoying life.

We were entering, as someone called it, "uncharted territory."

Jamie was reveling in life. He was feeding on the attention we were pouring into him. Suddenly, none of the other cats were getting any time from us. It was all about Jamie and there was little time for anything else. In a big nod from the universe, I had no freelance work. I was grateful for this. Time had opened up so I could care for Jamie and take advantage of every precious moment.

Chris and I talked and talked. We were exhausted and we were going to be even more so. We had no idea what was coming down the road. We didn't want Jamie to suffer, we agreed. But here was where it got tricky. Because it did not seem that he was suffering. We watched him closely, daily, continuously. We were overjoyed to see any normal behavior. Were we tuned in, or in deep denial?

Jamie was one of the strongest willed cats I've ever known. I had no doubt that Jamie would will himself to live forever, if he could.

Here was a cat who was purring, interacting with us, cuddling, and obviously enjoying life.

And the voice of doubt crept in again. Who doesn't want their pet to live forever? Who wouldn't want to believe that their animal would try to live forever?!

I was crazy. If there was anyone that looked for meaning, and anthropomorphized, it was me.

Still, we watched. And Jamie, who was thriving in all the attention he was getting (he always wanted to be an only cat), suddenly shone.

Later, much later, these instances of Jamie's joy would be an incredible memory we would hold onto forever. In the midst of this crisis, all we could do was observe, note, take joy in the good things, and try to put together a constantly shifting big picture. What was the story? We were trying to figure it out.

Three days after the initial vet visit, I didn't call my vet back. I didn't want to take Jamie in for euthanasia. I didn't think he was ready.

Soon after, another vet pointed out to me that hydrating Jamie would be easier (and safer) using Lactated Ringer's solution. I went to my local vet (fifteen minutes down dirt roads that were straight and a little less remote than the drive to Ely). This vet and his vet tech taught me how to give subcutaneous fluids—a skill that put me on edge at first but gradually got easier. I was shown how to grab Jamie's skin, pull it up like a tent, and put the needle in the wide part (the base) of the tent. It was hard to get used to poking Jamie at first, and sometimes, the needle came out the side of the skin. The best places to do this on the body were where there was a lot of skin to grab. I was squeamish, but that would quickly fade out of necessity. The poking didn't bother Jamie at all.

A schedule—busy yet providing some organization around the chaos—was formed. Jamie was fed three times a day and given a total of 100 cc of Lactated Ringer's solution daily. The local vet was careful to point out this was palliative care. I agreed, and was happy that it seemed to be making Jamie alert, responsive, and interested in life. He seemed not to be suffering. We started to keep a journal.

"Look, Chris," I said. "Jamie is riding shoulders!" Down into the journal it went. Jamie had always loved to ride our shoulders. From very early in life, Jamie figured out how to climb on our shoulders, lie down, and drape himself around our necks like a scarf so he wouldn't fall off. He loved this and he really loved it now. Jamie was giving us vigorous head butts all day long, and he was purring continuously. I reminded myself that the meaning of the purr was not completely understood. Still, he seemed so happy.

As for me, I was on autopilot. My first waking thoughts were of Jamie. When I fell asleep I thought of Jamie. I have the ability to compulsively focus on one thing. This is what drove me. Outside, the

Surrendering Control

Today I learned just how much of a control freak I am. I borrowed my neighbor's old truck to go get some donkey manure (for our garden) from a friend's farm about forty-five minutes away. I got to the farm and parked the truck on the driveway. When I went to start the truck again to back it down to the barn, it wouldn't start.

So my neighbor said he'd come out and tow the truck home. It never occurred to me that I would have to sit in the dead truck and steer it all the way home. When that sank in, I started to get a little panicky.

If you've ever done this, it's dicey and a little intense. A lot intense, actually. There's a tow rope connecting the two trucks. The truck I'm "driving" is in neutral and the motor is off (obviously, since the truck is dead). It's a real art to keep the dead truck the right distance from the towing truck. And it takes a lot of trust.

I had to lightly tap the brakes when I wanted to slam them. I had to make sure that rope never got too slack, or I might ram into the truck in front of me. Faster curves in the road were freaky; downhills were worse. I've never concentrated so hard in my life on two things—the visible yellow tow rope between the two trucks, and keeping my foot right over the brake, ready to "lightly tap" and fighting the urge to slam the brakes. Everything I could stress out about, I did—the narrow country roads with no shoulders, the fact that my truck wanted to sway out in the middle of the road for some reason, the light rain that made it harder to see the tow rope, cars coming in the opposite direction.

We had to work in sync, and I had to completely surrender control. I was amazed at how hard it was.

You know this feeling when your animal companion is ill or toward the end of life. There may be very little you can control. It feels like you want to freak out about anything, everything. But really, in some situations, all you can do is trust. Work in sync with your animal companion. Be ready for the turns in the road, the uphills, and the downhills. Trust and surrender control.

weather was beautiful. I only noticed when I took Jamie out. If the sun was shining, I didn't think of taking a walk. I let Jamie stroll around on the grass. I gardened and got my hands in the dirt. It was a deadline that couldn't be ignored with our short growing season. Stuff had to get in the ground. But I was once or twice removed from everything I did—except anything involving my twenty-year-old orange cat.

Jamie's dream of being the "only cat" was finally coming true. The rest of the cats were being ignored while we focused on Jamie and his care. Jamie got nightly bedroom privileges. Daily, at 4:30 a.m., he woke my husband by pawing repeatedly at Chris's face.

"Get up. I want to eat!" was what the paw in the face meant.

We smiled, knowing this meant Jamie was still Jamie and still firmly in this life. Anything that showed us a normal, interacting Jamie—we treasured.

Jamie slept between our heads at night, purring at all hours. We normally didn't let any of the cats in the bedroom when we slept, but with Jamie, we gave him whatever he wanted.

My husband had a theory that Jamie wanted to be human. I thought so, too—Jamie loved us and wanted very little to do with the rest of the cats. I created a cat fantasy novel that revolved around Jamie coming back as a human in his ninth life.

Jamie and I spent a lot of time outside. I began to appreciate a cat's enjoyment of the outdoors. Soft wind riffled through Jamie's medium-length orange hair. His eye squinted shut in what looked like dreamy happiness and he raised his nose to the wind. He walked on our green lawn between the few fruit trees we had planted. I let him walk and walk. I decided there was nothing nicer than watching a cat walk outside. Jamie seemed more interested in moving around outside than in our small house. So I took the hint and gave him outside time every day, when possible. Sometimes he was out several times a day. Exercise surely must contribute to health, I reasoned.

Jamie and I sat by a newly planted apple tree. Five-foot-tall cages surrounded each fruit tree to keep the deer away. Chris and I worked hard to get those trees in the ground, digging into recalcitrant clay soil. Later that year, in the fall, we got eleven indescribably deli-cious apples from our two apple trees.

"Ka–chuck–a-chuck-a-chuck-a . . ." I whispered into Jamie's ear. He purred. I blew softly into his ear. Occasionally during his life, he blew into my ear, and it seemed to be an expression of love. So I was hoping he understood the meaning when I breathed gently into his ear.

I sang to Jamie too, outside and in. Many of our cats have their own songs, which are nonsensical, just like their nicknames. Jamie had two songs; this one:

I wanna go to the dry Tortugas!
Tuega Tuega Tuega! Tuega Tuega Tuega!

And:

Down in the west Texas town of Tortuga
Jamie Laredo was playing around.
He was a good boy and we loved him dearly
He always had all his paws on the ground.

Jamie purred as I sang. The sun shone and warmed my shoul-ders. There seemed to be a little hope among the craziness. Amidst the grief and the stress, and care-giving and the tiredness, there were many exquisite moments of joy.

I HAD TO TRAVEL for yoga teacher training. I'd lose over a thousand dollars if I cancelled. Nonetheless, I almost didn't go.

"Go," said amazing Chris. "I'll take care of stuff here." I won-dered if Chris realized what he was promising. It was a busy household in the best of times, and Jamie's care was quite time-consuming. It was akin to round-the-clock hospice care. I had dread in my stomach, and some relief too, to be going to a beautiful ashram in California where I've been before, to get what would be top-notch yoga training. I was traveling with a yoga teacher friend who was a cat lover, like me, and who knew down to the detail what was going on with Jamie.

But stress snuck up on me and came out sideways. As my friend Wende and I waited for our plane in the small Duluth airport, I realized I'd forgotten my allergy drops, two hours away at home. Chris mailed them but they didn't reach me until four days later at the retreat center. By the third and fourth day on retreat in the California mountains, my body was doing what I could only describe as a slow burn. I had inflammation building deep within—a foreign sensation.

Two flights and one shuttle ride later, Wende and I arrived at the retreat center and settled in. It was good to be back at this peaceful place in the Sierra Nevada mountains of northern California. But I called Chris daily, sometimes twice daily. I emailed constantly. It was several nights before I finally started to let go and relax a little.

Back at home, Jamie was having his up and down days. Decline (even though I couldn't bear to think of it in those terms yet) was a process with peaks and valleys. Now, I knew what people meant when they were referring to a very ill or terminal person, and they said, "She had a good day," or "He had a bad day."

Every good day I heard about sent me on a roller coaster of joy. Jamie would live! He'd made it another day. We took insane happiness in the most minute details of Jamie's life.

"Jamie played with a green bean." "Jamie chased a squirrel!" "Jamie purred all night on the bed and gave me head butts all night. He kept me awake!"

And the downers plunged us both into sorrow and despair. If there was a day where Jamie seemed to be sleeping too much, or didn't have the desire to get up, we worried. We wondered if the life force was going, or if Jamie was just having a down day. We wondered what was next. It was the most excruciating process. No one knew how it was going to go.

From the retreat center, I called my husband from a small wood-interior phone booth for Jamie-reports. The smell of pleasant chemical-free cleaner wafted through the beautiful reception building where people checked in. The people who belonged to this community had a look of peace and joy and poise. I wanted that now, but my innards boiled slowly without the allergy antigen drops that my body had become accustomed to. My skin, always sensitive and super-prone to eczema, flared and wouldn't subside. My neck was raw and red. I couldn't hide my stress and distress, no matter how poised I tried to look.

Cell phone reception at the retreat center was quite spotty in the mountains. Aside from the phone booths in the reception building, the other option was to take a fifteen-minute hike up a hill. There, an amazing vista looked out over fields and mountains. Sometimes I hiked up there to call Chris, get the updates on Jamie, and breathe. I cried, and I laughed if Jamie had done something funny that Chris was telling me about.

The training was good, and intense, and when we were in class, I was able to forget about home for a moment here and there. But the situation always pushed through my thoughts. I feared Jamie might pass on while I was gone, even though we had no reason to think he was at that stage. I was enjoying the training, and the California land was healing me with its peace. I stared at irises and butterflies while I ate breakfast outside in silence. I walked and walked through fields and up hills and on mountain trails.

A classmate and I took an early four-mile walk, daily, before breakfast and classes started. We took a dirt road route that traveled from the retreat center land onto the adjacent acreage of the Ananda intentional community, and back. The retreat center and the intentional community were founded by followers of Paramahansa Yogananda, and they live a yogic lifestyle to this day. We walked through woods, past the occasional home, saw the mountain vista when the topography opened up and gave us a view. We passed a goat farm and a big community garden. The California air and temperature was perfect in the early morning, in June.

My blonde classmate was from Reno and had the look of a western women who loved to be outside. She talked about a cat she

Catherine Holm

loved and lost. I told her I was worried that I wouldn't know the right time to take action. Linda told me the story of her cat.

She said her cat was old, and ill, eighteen years. Linda couldn't let go. The cat would cry and make discordant singing sounds. It seemed to be trying to tell her something. My friend took the cat to an animal psychic, who said that this was the cat's special song. Linda began to sing back to the cat. When it became apparent it was time for the cat to pass on, Linda made the appointment. The cat (who normally hated to get into a cage) walked right into her cat carrier. She died peacefully in my friend's arms at the veterinary office. Animals face death more courageously than we do.

My trip home was a blur. I had one thought on my mind—getting home to Jamie. Traveling from where I live (two hours from a small airport; four hours from a major airport) took effort and time. It was past midnight when I pulled into our house. It was clear and moonless and bright stars filled every bit of the sky. I went right into the house, and went right to Jamie, who was sitting on

Guilt Serves No Purpose

I can think of a few times when I've felt guilt in regards to my relationships with my cats. In both these cases, guilt served no useful purpose.

My first two cats were adopted together from a Humane Society. The elderly woman who had to surrender them for adoption had stipulated they be adopted together, since they were buddies. I was originally more attracted to Cleo (a short-haired gray and white cat) rather than Tigger (a long-haired cream-colored cat with blue eyes). Though Tigger had the more striking appearance, Cleo had more endearing qualities. Cleo hugged me around the neck with her paws. Tigger was withdrawn and depressed and barely made the effort to interact.

But life has a way of giving us interesting surprises. In two weeks, Cleo died of complications from suspected chronic pancreatitis. In the coming weeks, months, and years, my relationship with Tigger deepened and I learned to love this gentle and wonderful cat. She became one of my greatest teachers.

Did I look back and feel guilty that I'd ignored Tigger at first? Yes.

Was the guilt pointless and useless? Yes.

Sometimes we have to go through an experience to get to the other side of a lesson.

When my cats have been ill and at the end of their lives, it's an extremely bittersweet time. It's sweet because some of our deepest bonds are formed with our animals at this time. It's "bitter" because we know they are leaving and there's nothing we can do about it. And guilt can creep in, too. Guilt that maybe we feel closer to the animal since we know they are leaving. Guilt that we may not have paid them enough attention when they were healthier. But to me, when I look at it honestly, the guilt doesn't seem as pure as the bitter or the sweet. It seems smaller, and not as genuine. And I think this is true. Again, what's its purpose?

Instead of letting guilt pull us down, let's celebrate the wonderful. Instead of feeling guilty about things in the past we can't change, let's celebrate each moment with our cats, our animals, our relationships, our life. Love your cat now, even if the time is bitter or sweet. Like one of my yoga teachers said, go to the joy instead of the guilt in a situation. Let your cats help you.

the couch in the living room. Jamie visibly perked up, and purred continuously. I stayed up until 2:00 a.m., petting Jamie and telling him I missed him so much. We took him into the bedroom.

"He missed mama," said Chris. I fell asleep with my hand on Jamie and I kept it there all night. In the morning, Jamie woke Chris up at 4:30 a.m., pawing my husband's face. Time for feeding.

I WAS ETERNALLY GRATEFUL I had so little work that summer, even though the income was needed. I was barely aware of life outside Jamie and spent all my time with him. He actively watched me and wanted me in his sight. When it was sunny out, I took him outside and he sat in the grass, watching me garden. I took him into the office. He climbed in his favorite chair and napped. Otherwise, he laid on my yoga mat and soaked up the sun from a southern window. When I came over to the yoga mat to meditate, he crawled into my lap. It was as if he knew his days were numbered, and he wanted to make the most of every minute.

I've had glimpses of purity in my life when I feel I might be becoming the best possible human I can be. This was one of those times. Giving escalated between Chris, me, and Jamie. We would do anything for each other. We were giving to Jamie. He was giving to us. There was a highly spiritual sense about all this, I told my husband. Chris didn't argue, though he was not quite as interested in spirituality as I was, and called himself an atheist.

I saw what was going on as a mountain of love, being built layer by layer. Jamie gave to us, we gave to Jamie. When I wondered how Jamie could possibly show us any more love, he found another way.

I was carrying him around in the yard one day. It was sunny and we were walking by the pond on my left. Across the small pond was visible a forest of tamarack and spruce. The forest was our land and eventually abuts state forest land. I held Jamie and brought his head close to mine. He turned toward me, in my arms, and sniffed gently into my ear, as if he was blowing.

"Oh, sweetie," I whispered, holding him closer. I felt my heart could turn inside out with all the love I wanted to show him. There was a bittersweet urgency to all this. I wanted to love love love him, because I knew that someday, he would not be here to love. I wanted him to know, from his ears to his paws to his tail, in his every cell, how much we loved him. It was a tender bond and though it was stretching, I felt his will. He was doing everything to postpone or delay the breaking of the bond.

I HAD TO TRAVEL again that summer. This obligation would have been difficult to get out of—I was reading from my book in upstate New York, and two of my friends there were collaborating with me on the event. I'd read, and they'd fold what I'd read into a Yoga as Muse™ presentation. (Yoga as Muse is something we'd all been trained to lead workshops in—a way to use the tools of yoga to help people tune into their creativity.) We'd put a lot of work into this and I needed to be there.

Prior to Jamie's illness and care, Chris and I would have made this upcoming trip part of our annual visit to Vermont. My book-reading event in New York would have been folded into our Vermont trip. But one of us needed to stay here to care for Jamie. I checked into going out east alone, lucked out on a ridiculously cheap airfare, and headed out to upstate New York for five days to do my reading.

It would be a fast trip, and Jamie seemed to be doing well. Still, I worried. We were still hydrating Jamie five times a day, and still feeding him three times a day. He seemed to be holding his own. He was thin, and it was difficult to get enough food into him with a syringe. It was crazy, and we didn't have the money, but I found myself wondering about a feeding tube. Jamie seemed to have such a will to live. I knew this was done for animals and I had experience with a cat with one. But it was not a smart financial reality. Worse, I didn't know if the University of Minnesota hospital would consider putting a feeding tube in a twenty-year-old cat.

We started adding a high calorie supplement to Jamie's food, and we also, upon the recommendation of one of the vets, fed him high calorie prescription food. This food, the vet tech told me, was often used for animals that were in serious medical trouble and needed to get calories into their bodies.

The New York trip was fun and again, a landscape far from home. The Hudson River Valley in upstate New York is a verdant, magical place. It's alive with culture, and there's the awareness that New York City is never far away. But there's also a beautiful rural flavor and some of the prettiest countryside I've ever seen. People there seemed to have a real zest for life and are interested, and interesting. I walked daily down paved and dirt country roads and saw some amazing scenery—creeks, green hills, tall lush trees, vines I didn't recognize. Humidity hung heavy in the air and I sweated constantly. Tucked in the country, billionaires had homes with indoor horse stables and riding rings. Right down the road from the billionaire's home, a small and nondescript house was in need of repair. Tattered laundry hung from a frayed line off the side of the house. A brook babbled over rocks across the street. My friend told me that an old man with twenty cats lived in this house. New York is a place of lush nature, and of extremes.

My friend and I walked across the Hudson River on a bridge exclusively for pedestrians. The bridge was accessed near a renovated train station in Poughkeepsie, where commuter trains come and go throughout the day. Way below the bridge, the surface of the Hudson was silver and blue, ripping with low waves that the wind played upon.

In the middle of the bridge, a bride and groom were being photographed by a professional photographer. "Less of your butt," yelled the photographer to the groom. "More of her!" Passersby laughed. "Yeah, man," someone called. This was New York, a far cry from reserved northern Minnesota.

AT THE NEW YORK AIRPORT, I found that my flight home was delayed a day because of bad weather in Detroit where I would be changing planes. I got to spend another night in upstate New York at my friend's house. We took a yoga class at a welcoming studio in an old building in Rhinebeck. Rhinebeck is a cute town, and the place where Chelsea Clinton was married.

Arriving home was a relief. As mixed as my feelings have been about living here, it's mostly veered to the good. I am always happy when I pull into the driveway. If the sun is out, our log house glows. I was happy to see the expanse of the forest again, and the calmness of a non-busy dirt road, after several days in the busy Hudson Valley.

Jamie was alive, and seemed well. The garden was in full swing, green and successful. Even the pepper plants—my greatest challenge in this place with such a short growing season—were looking healthy and at about the right stage. Our garden and woods didn't have the lush look of the Hudson River Valley, but we didn't have the humidity. In New York, the floors of my girlfriend's home felt as if they were sweating.

Chris was delighted to see me. We were both relieved I was back. There is a lot of work to keeping our house and land, especially in the non-winter times when there is so much to do outside. Normally I would have hit the ground running, anxious to work in the garden or do any of the outside things that needed done. This time, though, the situation with Jamie took precedence.

It was not until I'd been home a day or two, and settled in, that Chris revealed his own grief to me. Jamie had some down days while I was gone. There were days when Jamie seemed more depressed and lethargic. Chris didn't tell me because he wanted me to enjoy my trip, not worry, and have a good book event. My heart went out to Chris upon learning this. I could easily imagine how it is to be alone with a declining member of the family. It was very hard for Chris, who has a tough time expressing his grief. Chris wanted to be strong and he broke down.

There are times, when caring for a declining loved one, that grief hits you in the gut with no warning. Grief becomes a tsunami. This has happened to me, and this is what happened to Chris while I was gone. He pulled through it—they both did. But Jamie was always happiest when we were both home. Jamie was always happiest about being on the bed when we were both in the bed. There was a part of Jamie that seemed to be all about family. Family for Jamie was Chris, me, and Jamie. He could take or leave (probably leave) the other cats.

The other five cats were doing the best they could through this process. They went about their business; played, ate, napped, and watched us through narrowed eyes. They seemed to be leaving Jamie alone, for which I was grateful. Jamie still hissed at them. He was never going to be one who snuggled with the others. He was number one and had been for a long time. The others didn't cross him.

I was glad to be home, and had no plans to travel any time soon. I settled into the unknown, breathing. Sometimes evenly, sometimes shakily, sometimes with fear. My feelings were there and I didn't deny them. I only marveled at the complexity of all of us—cats, humans, family—and how the letting go of one loved being brought up the best and the hardest of everything about this life.

Jamie, the king of his castle.
(Courtesy of Deborah Sussex Photography.)

Ours for a Short Time

We know nothing is permanent. We know this logically. But when it comes time to depart from permanence, we rebel. We want to stop death. Nothing stops death. Yet we try. It is the ultimate display of human stubbornness and will.

Never do I realize how much stubbornness and denial I have within myself until it comes to matters of death. I'll do anything, anything, to stop its march. I wonder, will I be as stubborn when it comes to my death? Will I rail and fight and hang on? Will I have a hard time going? Or is it harder for me to let others go?

How can such a bond be broken? It boggles my mind. How can the bond, the relationship, be there, then gone? It's the ultimate mystery I can't wrap my head around. Why are we so attached to the material? Think of the suffering (our own) that would be lessened or dissolved if we didn't try to understand death, if we didn't hang on—if we simply let go. I'm not sure I'm capable of it. If I ever reach this point of nonattachment, I'm sure I will be more spiritually evolved than I am now.

Two friends of mine had a farmhouse on forty acres of land in the scenic, beautiful, ecologically diverse bluff country of southeastern Minnesota. With strong environmental ethics of their own, they named the land and home "Ours for a Short Time." That has stayed with me.

We own nothing. Nothing is permanent. The land is ours for a short time, perhaps an almost invisible amount of time in the huge span of existence. My cats, my dogs, my companions, my lover and partner—are mine for a short time. Life and our time together is precious, something my loved cats and dogs have continually taught me. I am not the best student, and I don't always remember or get it right. But at the very least, I am learning to love better.

Parents pray they'll never see their children die. But those of us with animal companions will likely see these companions pass on. We get the lesson of "ours for a short time," even if we have to keep learning it over and over and over again. It's a lesson full of love, intensity, grief and pain—and strangely, perhaps one of the greatest gifts our animals give us. For I believe that their passing has made me realize that yes, I can love; yes, I can be a decent human; yes, I can serve them and be there for them, giving them what they need, no matter how hard, no matter how painful.

Target's Drive Home

My cell phone rang as I sped from our northern Minnesota home to the Twin Cities. Target, my ten-year-old black cat, sat next to me in a rigid cat carrier. I had to keep watching the speed limit because I kept blowing over it—not my usual style of driving. I had a lot on my mind, and cat health issues will bring me to a stressful place just as quickly as some of life's other challenges.

My husband was on the other end of the phone. "How's Target?" he said, in a tight voice. His voice sounded as tight as my heart felt.

"He's being cute."

I don't think it was possible for Target not to be cute, even within the confines of a small cat carrier, on the way to risky surgery. Target looked at me and chattered, as he always did. Chris and I had long suspected this black cat had some Siamese in him. Though he had a square face that didn't resemble that breed, he had the long slim legs of a Siamese, and he talked incessantly. When Target talked, his stunning green eyes fixed on you and didn't let you go.

Trees whizzed by on the sides of Minnesota I-35, and the forest gradually transitioned from boreal to deciduous as I drove south. The fire in Target's eyes helped me feel hopeful about what we were speeding toward in the cities.

"Call me when it's over and Target's come through it," Chris said. My husband was choosing words carefully and I was glad. We were embarking on a risky procedure—surgery for a cancerous tumor on the intestine. Target's weight was down and he had not been able to eat. If this surgery was going to happen, it needed to happen now.

Through the wire door of the cat carrier, Target butted his head against my fingers. I would often ride this way with cats—keeping one hand against the door of the cat carrier so they would know I was there if they wanted a pet or a head butt.

Seven years prior to this drive to the cities, I had adopted Target from our regional Humane Society. I loved to volunteer there and play with the cats. I wasn't looking for a cat. (Isn't that what we always say?) I had my hands full at home with Milo, Jamie, Kali, and Karma. The mix was working fine (with the exception of Jamie who really always wanted to be the only cat, and who only tolerated Milo) and I wasn't about to introduce an unknown variable.

But Target grabbed my heart. On a day when I was volunteering at our local shelter, I'd made time to take each and every cat into the "cat room." At least thirty to forty adult cats were up for adoption that day. I took each cat out of their cage and into the bigger "cat room" to play with them. Here I could drag a toy, brush the cats, or simply cuddle them, depending upon what that cat seemed to want most.

Sleek, black Target loved it all. And when I went to put him back in his cage, he wouldn't let go. He wrapped his paws around my neck and hugged me, holding on.

I am always stunned when this happens, especially when it comes from a cat I didn't necessarily notice at first. And Target was one of those cats. I hadn't noticed him. I had never really noticed black cats, and had never had one.

So I took the hint. I did not put him back in his cage right away. I played with him more. The more time I spent with him, the more he captivated me. Target had humor and he was a communicator. He wanted to connect and made every effort possible to let a person know that he was there, he was listening, and he wanted to talk. All of this was done in an insistent, intelligent voice.

I called the Humane Society every few days to see if Target was still up for adoption. I wanted him, but I hesitated to add another cat to our crowded home. The staff was onto me.

Amazingly, no one adopted Target. Now that I was in love with him, I thought he'd get snapped up by someone else aware enough to

Driving with Cats

Cats Live in the Moment

My cats don't tense up, waiting for the other shoe to drop. They don't worry about their luck running out. They live in the moment, enjoying their naps, their play, their meals, the attention we give them. We could learn a thing or two from them.

The last few years have been pretty good to me. But every once in awhile, I catch a negative or cautious thought trying to sneak in:
· "Enjoy the good because it won't always be good..."
· "What goes up must come down . . ."
· "Enjoy this while it lasts . . ."
· "You're so lucky . . ."

I credit yoga and awareness for helping me catch these thoughts before they turn into something more. I mean—Why? "What goes up must keep going up" could be just as true as "What goes up must come down," so why not pick the more positive statement? It improves my mood, which may even affect the likelihood of more good stuff happening.

I said to my husband today, "I'm really feeling very lucky." But he said, "Luck has nothing to do with it. You worked hard for years." Actually, I think the truth is somewhere in between.

Chester gets up in the morning. He doesn't entertain the thought of luck running out. Chester jumps on the bed, purrs, sticks his fat-cheeked face up to ours, and gives us a "murph." ("Murph" is a little sound he makes when he's hungry.) He's enjoying the moment. Getting rid of stingy thinking helps me enjoy the moment, and the life, more.

see Target's attributes. But perhaps black cats are like black dogs—there are so many of them that they get overlooked in favor of a stunning calico, or some other beautiful cat.

Target turned out to be one of the most extroverted, people-oriented cats I'd ever met. His rescue story matched his personality—the Humane Society staff named him Target because he was rescued when he managed to get into the local Target department store. It was cold out, he had likely been abandoned, and the store was warm and had Target's favorite beings—people!

A month after first meeting Target, I adopted him and brought him home.

For several wonderful years, we had a blast with Target. Target loved company and would run to the door and enthusiastically greet anyone with his Siamese-y, unforgettable voice. He danced with us and loved to wrestle. We'd play MC Hammer on the computer, running a YouTube video. As we danced in the kitchen, Target would dance with us—racing back and forth on the counter, following us, eyes alive.

If we'd been gone and came back home, we could always count on Target's face peering through the front door window. He'd talk to us in his insistent, demanding voice—"Get in! Hurry up! I want company!"

50

As a huge bonus, Target's introduction to the household was one of the easiest I've ever seen. He got along with everybody in very short order. I'd feared that Milo (the number one, dominant cat) might hand Target his head. But the introduction of Milo and Target was quick and successful, if accidental. Milo slipped into the bedroom where we'd temporarily housed Target. I was folding laundry on the bed and I froze, waiting for the cat fight, the howling, the hissing, the flying fur. Instead, Target flopped down easily on his side, looking at Milo with an expression of happiness, or flirtation, or both. And Milo, my tough street cat, didn't raise a paw. He sat down and began grooming Target. They groomed each other. Such was the energy of Target—he moved through life happily and easily, and he got along with everyone. Target was a born collaborator.

Carol, my good friend and fellow cat lover, adored Target. She and her husband, on vacation, found a piece of folk art and bought it for me. It's a large framed poster of a slightly silly looking black cat holding a package of cheese with a picture of another black cat's head on the cheese package. The caption under the poster reads: "Chat Noir—Fantastique!" Every time I look at that poster, I grin. It so perfectly captures the clownishness, ease, and good nature of all the black cats I have come to know, starting with Target.

My STRESSFUL DRIVE to the cities with Target had been predicated by developments six weeks prior. At that time, my extroverted and vocal cat started to change, subtly. He would sit in the empty bathtub for no reason. He grew quieter. And he started to eat less and lose weight. Target was ten years old, and I was not ready for him to be ill. But as I learn over and over again, I have no control over anything. Will I ever truly learn this and have it stick? Will I ever completely accept it and grow easy with it? I don't know.

I got to the vet's office in the cities and Target clung to me. That unnerved me, as well as the fact that it felt chaotic in this normally calm and pleasant lobby that was all about cats. I signed a release and I left, to wait. And wait. I was to call back in four hours.

Whenever I make these trips back to the Twin Cities, I feel increasingly like an outsider. I grew up in these cities but I am no longer that comfortable in them. Suburbs, such as the one I traveled to for Target's surgery, are even worse. They are sprawling, and cars and chain restaurants dominate the landscape.

Stressed out over waiting for Target to get through surgery, I did not know what to do. I made a reservation at a local hotel (I would need to spend one night in the suburb with Target, who would be too weak to make the four hour drive home in the same day). I paced. I sat in the car as the time got closer to when the vet would call me. I wrote a poem to Target, calling him the "Target of my Heart." I drew a heart with a target inside it.

My cell phone rang and I answered, my heart hammering in my throat.

"He made it," said the vet.

Shakes traveled down my body faster than waterfalls. I could not move. The gray waters of White Bear Lake stretched into the horizon.

The vet instructed me to wait another four hours, and come back to the office at 2:00 p.m. At that time, I'd be given post-op instructions for Target, including the treatment of his incision. A huge weight slid off my chest and I dared to believe life was right again.

Celebration was in order. I cannot eat when I am stressed but with the stress now gone, I treated myself to a bagel concoction at one of those suburban chain eateries—something I usually never eat (too caloric and too full of wheat and gluten). I decided I really needed a massage for stress relief and I went to the phone book. Surely, in these populated suburbs, some massage therapist might have a walk-in opening. In luck, I located a massage therapist with an opening. I drove across the sprawling suburb to yet another strip mall, where a generic-looking storefront advertised massage therapy services. Parking, I started to get out of the car, anticipating the pleasure of healing hands on tight stressed muscles, and ultimate relaxation.

My phone interrupted me again, with its quiet, frog ringtone.

The vet spoke in a low and quiet voice. "His heart is giving out," she said.

No guarantees.

I sped out of the parking lot, cursing the distance I'd put between me and the vet clinic. I shouldn't have gone so far away! How could these damn suburbs be so big? What was this damned sprawly-ness eating up the earth? Stress turned into anger and fear. I gripped the steering wheel. The gods were on my sides as I met no police cars, or I surely would have gotten a ticket. I pulled up to the vet clinic, legs shaking, and stumbled in. A kind receptionist quickly guided me downstairs, where surgeries were done. I held my Target, whom they had kept alive with oxygen until I could get there. I held Target as he passed.

THE STAFF AT THIS CLINIC love and know cats. And they knew me. They knew I had a long drive back. They did not rush me. The vet had a house call to make and the staff offered me the exam room, to sit with Target for as long as I needed.

This exam room, which I've been in many times, has been equipped with cats in mind. The windows have wide sills that cats can sit on. Catnip toys are here and there on the floor. A small wooden cat figurine sits in one corner. It's the size of a cat and I'm told the feline patients swat it, either thinking it's real or just trying to show it a thing or two.

There was a small bench in this room—one of those benches that you might put in a home entryway with a compartment for storing scarves and mittens, and a place to sit to pull on boots. On this bench, I sat with Target on my lap.

Tears flowed. I didn't care about how I looked, or have any awareness of how I sounded or what I might have said to Target. I sat there for a good hour, holding my cat. I am sure I talked to him, and told him how much I loved him. My heart was ripped open in that horrible and profound way we feel when we are grieving.

And at some point, Target's black fur lost its disheveled look. At some point, in that misty, muddy, uncertain one hour when I sat with my cat, Target began to glow.

It was a subtle thing, and probably something that perhaps I'd not be equipped to notice, were I not stripped down by grief. This is the real gift of grief—it bulldozes you out of your own way. Target glowed. His fur came alive. I felt a subtle rumbling energy from his body. I have felt the same thing when other beloved animals have passed. I am not sure what it is.

I drove the four hours home with Target beside me. I cried most of the way, stroking him. I had placed him in the bottom of the cat carrier, on plastic padding from the vet's office. The top of the carrier had been removed and discarded in the back seat. I told Target how wonderful he was.

I stopped at a wayside pull-off area to use the bathroom but I could not bear to leave Target alone in the car. I rested my forehead against the steering wheel and I cried. I never believe how much crying I have in me. It reassures me in a strange way, and reminds me I am not numb—I am a person who can feel.

Chris met me as I pulled into the garage, once home, but he immediately focused on Target.

"My beautiful boy," he said, tears in his eyes.

"His heart gave out," I said, numb, now that I was home. For the moment, I was spent of tears. They would come again later.

"That's because his heart was too big to hold," said Chris. He meant it, and it was true. Everything about the experience pointed to heart—Target's big heart, my broken heart, Chris's grieving heart.

Such is the nature, and the immensity of the event, when such a bright spirit passes. We cannot quite wrap our heads or hearts around it.

CHRIS MADE A LOVELY CASKET, and we put Target's body in it that night. But we did not close the box. I wrote a love note and put it with Target, laying it next to his shiny fur. We scattered colorful flower petals next to him. To my eyes, he still glowed.

I slept on the floor that night, next to our bed, Target's open casket next to me. I kept my hand in the box all night and continually woke up, from sleep, to stroke his body. It was my way of hanging on, or letting go, or both.

TARGET'S DEATH WAS HARD for both of us; the surprise that had been dealt felt cruel and random. It had not been a slow goodbye, but fast and unexpected. There had not been time to say goodbye.

A few days later we escaped our surroundings and drove the two-and-a-half-day trip to Vermont. I cried much of the way out, and Chris said I looked the most exhausted he'd ever seen me look. We let the verdant green mountains of Vermont, and their rushing streams, heal us. We listened to the sound of the wind through the firs and the pines, and we watched the cool sun just starting to turn leaves to red and yellow and orange. We let Vermont into us; we let its landscape begin to soften and bring together our broken hearts.

A RED PITCHER MADE of Depression glass sits on a desk in our living room. The desk abuts the back of a futon. Cats love to be in high places and there are not too many high places in our home. One relatively higher place is along the top of the upright futon cushion. Cats of ours love to sit there, and Target had been no exception.

My home office is located behind our house. As I came out of my office one night, I saw the red vase through the window of the house. Tired from working, I looked at that pitcher and could have sworn I saw Target's head, just as it looked when he sat astride the vertical futon cushion. When I came into the house, I told Chris what I had seen.

Chris looked at me for a moment. "I saw that too," he said. "In here."

Target, our darling cat who was with us for too short a time, was to give us many more of these gifts. Sometimes animals leave right away. And sometimes they don't. With a cat like Target, the relationship is the thing. The connection matters, and the connection is real—in life, in death, and beyond.

Patience and Persistence, Berry Picking, and Working with Cats

We've been berry picking a lot in the woods the last few days. The raspberries are excellent this year and the blueberries are not bad.

Berry picking takes patience. With delicate and low blueberry bushes, you need to be gentle and slow. The berries are smaller than the grocery store variety, and they're often hidden under leaves. Raspberries are tricky in other ways—prickly branches, tall, and berries near the ground as well as up high. If the berries are ripe and you knock the bush a bit too hard, you're likely to lose a lot of berries to the ground.

Berry picking makes me think of Rama (a.k.a. Dyson Pointy Paws), our current black cat. We adopted him as an adult cat from our Humane Society (probably too soon) after our black cat Target unexpectedly passed away. We missed Target so much and we wanted a replacement. Not always a good idea, but that's where we were emotionally at the time: broken-hearted.

Rama looked exactly like Target but that's where the similarity ended. Target loved all people. Rama would only tolerate me. Target could be handled and rough-housed, and he reveled in it. Rama would nip or whine if anyone (including me) held him the wrong way. Target had a loud, talky voice. Rama barely purred.

I had the feeling that Rama was deeply insecure and untrusting, and that he needed to understand how things worked.

And so, like berry picking, I worked patiently and steadily with Rama. I taught him what was appropriate and what was not. I handled him gently, reading his body language, and slowly getting him comfortable with more and more touching.

Rama has come a long way. After almost two years in our household, he is secure and happy, well behaved and playful. Rama will never be Target. Our cats are unique and can never be replaced. But it means more than I can say when I pick up Rama, and he snuggles into me, leaning back his head, eyes shut in happy contentment, humming with a barely discernible purr. You almost need to be in the quiet woods of pine, spruce, birch, and berries to hear it.

Dane Lodge—du Nord Teaches Me

Since my book of short stories was published in 2010, I have become more public, though I still need my times to retreat. A year after Target's death, in 2008, I was still a fairly introverted person. On this one-year anniversary of Target's death, I was giving a writing workshop at a retreat for women at YMCA Camp du Nord on the edge of the Boundary Waters Wilderness.

Du Nord is an extraordinary place that has grown on me. In fact, as I wrote this in 2012, I was at du Nord, finally taking the two free nights offered to me in exchange for teaching that workshop. It brought back all sorts of memories and that's why I wrote this story of Dane Cabin and the one year anniversary of Target's death.

Prior to the 2008 workshop I gave, I had only been at du Nord once. A life coach friend and I had taken a retreat together in one of the tiny cabins, to coach each other and spend time in nature. Camp du Nord is located on forty-seven acres on Burntside Lake, one of the most beautiful northern Minnesota lakes, in my opinion, and one portage away from the Boundary Waters Wilderness.

My husband and I regularly wilderness camp in the Boundary Waters (or BWCA) and generally I'm not that interested in other kinds of "camping." I wasn't expecting much from du Nord, figuring it'd be a very civilized experience in the woods. It is—many of the camper cabins are nicer than our own house. However, the magic of du Nord worked on me that first time with my coach friend. In our tiny cabin, we watched as the winter ice began to melt off Burntside. White pines towered around our cabin and waved their soft needles in the wind, whispering like a magical higher power. The sound of the trees, the view of the lake, and the quiet of offseason du Nord worked on me that first time, and would work on me again.

At the 2008 fall retreat, I'd been asked to teach morning yoga and give a writing workshop. Several facilitators were giving different workshops throughout the day. The women at the retreat were from all over Minnesota, though many came from the Twin Cities. I could feel du Nord working on all of them.

When I wrote this story, I walked the many du Nord trails. I sat on a hill overlooking the lake. Surrounded by trees, with the pristine beauty of the lake in a panorama, I wondered for the first time if the trees knew how much I loved them. I wondered if I had ever thought to thank the trees before and to truly love them in their immensity. They were just as much a mystery to me as death is, or anything profound. They were as much a mystery to me as God may be to some.

In 2008, I had spent the first night of the retreat in a large cabin (called Greenstone) that housed most of the facilitators. "Cabin" is a misnomer—this beautiful structure would make a lovely home. (The word "cabin" is used loosely in Minnesota, and second homes or stunning lakeside mansions are usually called "cabins.") Because I was one of the last facilitators to arrive, my sleeping arrangements were not the greatest and were out in the open area of Greenstone Cabin. When I'm "on" all day, I do appreciate being able to close a door at night and have my own space, though I know this isn't always possible.

On the second day of the three-day retreat, my life coach friend, Thea, who was also facilitating, told me that she had to leave that day and I was welcome to stay in Dane Cabin, where she'd been housed. Dane Cabin had been given to her so she could run her workshop right in the cabin. Thea did a workshop where women made "spirit dolls" and the space of Dane Cabin allowed her to easily lay out all her materials. When her workshop was complete and she'd packed her stuff, I moved my stuff into Dane. Thea and I said our goodbyes and she drove back into town where she lives.

I was beginning to feel as if I needed a little down time. Facilitators are "on" all day at these retreats, even between their workshops. Meals are taken together in du Nord's beautiful new dining hall. The food is fabulous. I was looking forward to bed that night, but the after-dinner agenda looked too interesting to miss.

Two professional storytellers gave a phenomenal presentation on oral storytelling. We were all given the opportunity to try a little oral storytelling. As a writer, I was very interested. I began to see the power of this kind of expression, and it excited me. There is palpable power, and healing, and energy, in speaking words and stories aloud. Many of us were moved by this presentation.

I walked to Dane from the dining hall using a trail through the woods that passed several cabins, crossed a stream called "Moose Drool Crick," and went by a lakeside seating area (for worship services or presentations) called Burntside Stage. A huge totem pole marked the center of du Nord Village, and the dirt path/driveway to Dane Cabin was right next to the totem pole. I walked up to Dane, noting that the light next to the door was on, and wondering how that had come to be.

I opened the door to Dane and walked in, and felt . . . a different feeling. Not threatening, or dangerous . . . just different. That is the only way I can describe it.

Dane is constructed from hand-hewn logs and was built in 1933. It was the first lodge at du Nord and was where the founders of this camp (three women schoolteachers) lived as they developed their dream for a summer camp that would teach families and children about the wilderness. When you walk into Dane you walk immediately into a large living room area with a big window that faces the lake. A stone fireplace and some bunk beds are off to the right; a staircase and the kitchen and a bathroom are to the left. Abutting the kitchen is an attached, unheated enclosed room with a stone foundation and floor, which may have been used for cold storage.

Tired from the day, and at the same time infused with the power of oral storytelling, I walked upstairs with my sleeping bag to pick out a bed.

Again, I had that strange feeling of differentness. I don't have the language to put to this but I can only tell you what it was not: it was not distressing, not scary, not threatening—it simply *was*.

The hallway in the upstairs of Dane Lodge was narrow. (People were smaller in those days!) I chose a bedroom with a window that faced the lake, and I unrolled the bag on the blue camp-issue mattress, which was surprisingly comfortable.

That night, as I turned off all the lights and settled into bed, the lake glittered outside my window. The white pines and spruce, the birch, surrounded the house and held me. Du Nord and Dane Lodge began to work their magic.

Pulsing with the power of stories told out loud, I thought of Target. And I began to speak his story out loud, addressing it directly to him—my powerful, loving, people-person-cat whom I still grieved.

"Target," I began. "I met you at the Humane Society."

I breathed, taking something into my chest, something bigger than myself.

"I didn't notice you at first, but you held out your paws and grabbed me. You held on to me with your laser green eyes. You pulled me in, Target. You reached into my heart."

I spoke with rhythm and emphasis, as if I performed to an audience. I was performing for myself, and for Target.

I began to cry, but paid no attention to my tears, aware instead of the the power of words spoken out loud. On and on I went. Minutes passed. Hours passed. I channeled something. I had no idea what I was saying. I only knew that I was telling Target his story. I was telling the air his story. I was telling Dane Lodge his story. I was telling the universe his story. I was telling the story of all of us who grieve something we loved and lost.

I cried, and at the same time, I had an electric, alive feeling pulsing through the cells of my body. This was oral expression. This was another facet of storytelling. I felt I reached across something we do not understand, something that separates us, and does not. I was certain Target heard me. Wherever he was, wherever we go when we pass over—my words created a bond to his essence, whatever that essence was.

Spent, I fell asleep, the pillow moist with my tears, my body depleted, the lake and the pines and Dane Lodge protecting my dreams and my heart.

ON THE LAST MORNING, there was no yoga class on the retreat agenda. I used the time to stay at Dane Lodge. I did not want to leave. I skipped breakfast, knowing that a delicious final brunch would be served later in the morning. I did my own yoga and meditation practice in Dane Lodge's living room overlooking the lake. The pristine rocks and pines and spruce created the milieu that is so unique to Burntside. I understand now how those schoolteachers who founded du Nord were so taken with this lake.

I did very little *asana* (yoga posture), not wanting to move the furniture. It somehow didn't seem appropriate. Most of my yoga practice that morning involved breathing and meditating. I meditated for some timeless period, breathing and emptying my mind, turning my focus again and again to the lake, full of gratitude for the beauty of the woods, the lake, this camp, my emptying out the previous night.

A rustle from the kitchen startled me; a distinct noise like the movement of stiff clothing. What I thought of at the time was a floor-

Glass Half Full? Ask Your Cat!

This morning my husband was cutting up deer meat on the table for packaging. Deer season opened last Saturday and my husband got a deer on the first day right away in the morning—a real first after many years of hunting.

Chester, my orange cat, was very interested in the raw deer meat. Our cats really go nuts for raw game meat, such as the grouse and the venison that sometimes make it into our household. Chester sat at the table on a chair and could barely restrain himself. He was good and managed to resist getting on the table, but he couldn't hold back from taking a paw and gently, ever so quietly, raising it and moving it toward the meat . . . as if we couldn't see him.

Milo (deceased) also had a love for raw venison, but he was more aggressive about going after it than Chester has been. (Milo had a more edgy, "street-smart" personality and Chester is a softer, gentler cat.) In the weeks before his death, Milo grew increasingly picky about what he'd eat. I had to keep switching foods. Canned food was more appealing than dry food. My vet says that picky eating is often a common theme at the end of a cat's life. But in the last few weeks of Milo's life, when we were butchering that year's deer, Milo couldn't restrain himself. He gorged himself on meat scraps we gave him, even though he couldn't keep it down. I think he enjoyed every bite.

Instances like this remind me stories have several sides, and glasses can be half full or half empty. Though that time was a stressful time, and we knew Milo was on the decline, we also loved watching Milo being a cat and devouring venison. And we still smile about the memory now, years later.

length skirt or the sweep of a broom. Perhaps the sound was something else—but it was definite and it was there.

Spirit? I wondered. *Ghost.*

I felt no fear.

My items were packed and waiting. I told Dane Lodge *Namaste* (which means "the light in me greets the light in you"). I left Dane Lodge, wondering what had happened in that place.

LEAVING DU NORD AFTER the retreat, I stopped on the way home at the Front Porch in Ely, a local coffeehouse. My life coach friend Thea and her husband Dave happened to be there, and we chatted about du Nord and the retreat.

"Did you notice anything in Dane Lodge?" Thea asked.

I looked at her with surprise. I told her about the noise I'd heard. I told her how I'd been so moved the night before; how I poured out Target's story to Target and to the world and the sky.

They both looked at me with raised eyebrows.

"Oh," said Thea. "Lucky you! She made herself known to you. I wanted to sense her, but it didn't happen to me."

Thea explained that many believe that a spirit lives in Dane— one of the founding schoolteachers of du Nord that lived there.

It was my turn to be surprised and affirmed. What I had sensed could be real, and yet it had felt accepting, not dangerous. I wondered if the spirit had supported me as I cried out my story of Target. I wondered if the spirit had listened. Perhaps this would not have happened for me if I had not stayed in Dane Lodge. It was another step in healing through the grief process.

People tell stories of lights going on and off in Dane Lodge, or noises, or the floor creaking when no one else is in the building. The current caretaker at du Nord is a practical man with never-ending maintenance responsibilities. He poo-pooed any mention of ghosts, but said that his sister had a photo of people inside Dane, where an orb is present in the photo. His sister, and others, were convinced a ghost lives in Dane Lodge.

In 2012, I was sitting in another, newer, cabin at du Nord. The weather has many faces here; the day had seen sun, and snow showers that thankfully weren't sticking. The lake was gray and choppy. Each cabin had a book titled *YMCA Camp du Nord* with pictures and a story of du Nord's history. One of the teachers who founded du Nord was an English and Speech teacher. Perhaps she listened to me as I told the story of Target. Perhaps she made me, a fellow lover of words, welcome in Dane.

My husband Chris was with me when we used these nights at du Nord that I had been generously given. I took him on a walking tour of the entire camp. No one else was staying here, and the caretaker had told us that it was fine to peek in the cabins. There were twenty-eight cabins and each was unique.

I'd told Chris the story of Dane Lodge and he wanted to see it. As we walked up to Dane's front door the hair on the back of his neck went up. He felt it, too.

We went in and I showed Chris where I slept and told the story of Target. I showed Chris where I was sitting when I heard the noise, and where the noise came from. Chris liked Dane Lodge and it's at the top of his list for a cabin to stay in when we come back.

"*Namaste,*" I said, pressing palms together, bowing my head slightly in the direction of the living room. *Thank you for allowing us to visit.* We backed out of the front door and gently closed it.

Target, playing on the floor.
(Photo courtesy of the author.)

The Solstice Cat

In northern Minnesota, December can be mild (mild means temperatures in the thirties) or brutal (twenty below zero or lower). December is an unpredictable month. Minnesota natives expect January and February to be frigid, but December is a wild card.

On December 20, 2007, winter solstice, the daily forecast was heading in the brutal direction. Temps that night were predicted to hit thirty below. It barely got to one above zero in midday. The sun was low in the southern horizon; the air cold and dry; the sky bitter blue. Piles of snow made small mountains where Chris had snow-blown paths around our property. I was walking quickly from the house to the office and rounding the south side of the house (with deck) on one of our snow-blown paths. Our Christmas tree, a small spruce we'd taken from our field, twinkled in the French doors that opened from the living room to the deck.

I heard a plaintive cry from the deck and stopped in my tracks.

Our wood picnic table was stacked on end against the house for the winter. Against the underside of the table crouched a white cat. It cried again and huddled close to the house. Our house is a handcrafted log home, and the large logs hold a lot of heat. On the south side of the house they hold even more heat. The cat pressed against the house, but when I came closer it took off, running across the deck, jumping through the railing supports, and landing on the snow near our canoe. The cat crouched under the canoe, whining.

A cat wouldn't last out here long. And I sensed this cat was not outdoor savvy.

I ran to grab some food, hoping the cat had not turned too feral and I could get close to him.

I walked slowly toward the canoe, where the cat hid. I kept my arms close to myself, to avoid scaring him. I moved carefully, without a lot of noise, trying not to let my boots crunch on the cold dry snow.

"Come on, sweetie," I whispered. I held a yogurt container full of cat food and I rattled it. The cat lost all fear and shoved his face into the food.

I grabbed cat and food, and brought him into my warm office. It turned out the cat was nowhere near feral, and bonded to me right away, purring and letting his chin be scratched.

THE LAST THING I NEEDED was another cat. Five cats resided in our small house. I was also well aware of the expendable nature of cats where I live (and perhaps everywhere). Shelters are overrun with adult cats. Kittens or dogs seem to adopt more easily.

I got on the phone, calling every neighbor I could think of. I described the cat in detail—mostly white, with black tabby spots on his back, head, and hind legs; a tabby tail with a white tip; light green eyes; almost a pink albino cast to his skin. (Later, I would learn that the description for this cat's coloring is "domestic with black and white Van pattern." "Van" refers to a pattern in a cat's coloring where the cat is mostly white, with other markings.)

Being the optimist I am, I wanted to believe this cat had simply gotten out and had not been dumped on a cold winter day. But everyone said they knew nothing about this cat. I knew our regional shelter was full, and would also not help our town as our town did not pay for animal control services. I didn't have the heart to drop the cat off in the middle of the night at the shelter, even though the shelter provides cat carriers for these drop-offs.

I kept the cat, reasoning he'd stay in the office so the house wouldn't get any more crowded. The office is heated only with wood, and I worried it might get cold out there for him, but I also knew if a cat has shelter, they can survive cold up to a point. I made him a place to snuggle with warm blankets, and I heated the office as much as possible. This had benefits as it forced me to work in the office, rather than the house—even though it meant keeping two woodstoves running, rather than one.

At first, I called the cat Solstice Cat, but eventually, I named him Kieran. We determined with a vet visit that he was indeed a neutered male. Someone had been responsible enough to take care of that. It made me wonder if he'd been intentionally dropped at my house. *Never let a small town know you too well,* a cynical voice jibed me from within. But how is that possible? And I couldn't live with myself if I left an animal out in the cold to die.

Being a writer and pretty imaginative, I concocted stories in my head about Kieran's origins. I wanted to feel bad for the family that I had pictured had dropped him off. Perhaps they were in financial straits. Financial troubles were certainly prevalent, and the economic crisis was part of the reason local shelters were overrun. I was glad someone had the mindfulness to invest in neutering him. But to dump him, in the middle of winter, seemed unnecessarily cruel.

Kieran had his own dark demons, and it has been my experience that cats deal in different ways with whatever trauma they've been through. All the pads of his paws had been frostbitten, and the skin turned gray and sloughed off, leaving new pink skin. It hurt him to walk for a while. He also lost the tip of an ear to frostbite.

More strange were other behavioral aberrations, which I attribute to shock or trauma. Kieran appeared not to know how to, or had no desire to, look out a window. My small (sixteen-by-sixteen-foot) office has plenty of old recycled windows. Some work and some don't and I'd guess there's more window space than wall space. Many of the windows are at cat head level. Yet he showed no interest. I hoped this simply meant he'd had enough of the outside and didn't care to look at it again, for now. I hoped it didn't mean he'd lived in a closet or basement or a place without windows. I turned toward the future. With time and patience, a lot is possible.

Kieran also seemed not to know how to play. Most cats will chase a string or a toy or something that moves like prey—not this guy.

He did love to cuddle. And when I was in the office, he made it clear he wanted to be on my lap. I worked with him and hoped that in the future, he would enjoy things that other cats enjoyed, and hopefully, leave his demons behind.

A year later, I moved Kieran into the house. It was crowded with six cats, but Kieran wasn't getting enough exercise in the small office. Slowly, as I had done in the past, I integrated him over a period of a few weeks.

When Cats Come in from the Cold

I live in cold country—about an hour-and-a-half south of the Canadian border. Winter starts in October here, and sometimes doesn't truly leave until May. Frost is possible any given month. We sometimes get temps of forty below or worse. It's a tough, brutal, and deadly place for a cat to live outside—a cat without the option of shelter of some kind. Add to this that we live in a pretty remote rural area, surrounded by woods and a lot of predators. There aren't a lot of close outbuildings or garages or structures for a cat to hide in. The woods are full of wolves, fox, even some of the bigger cats.

Two of my cats, Karma and Kieran, showed up here either right at the onset of winter, or in the middle of winter. And what I noticed with them both is that it took them a while to learn to become easygoing cats. It seems that the experience of having to survive in the outdoors put any inherent playfulness or cute cat behaviors on the backburner.

Not that they were bad cats. It just took them both a long time to relax and learn to become housecats. I have no idea of their pasts, but neither one was feral.

Karma was solemn for the longest time. I had to teach her how to play with cat toys. We never let her get outside, because we have learned that if she gets out, she reverts to a type of wild and withdrawn behavior, as if she doesn't know us. And she becomes very skittish and almost impossible to catch.

Kieran was an even more extreme case. Though he's not afraid of the outside (and has been outside with me on a harness and lead), when he first came in, he acted as if he didn't know how to be a cat. Kieran showed no interest in looking out windows, even if squirrels raced across them or if birds flew by. He had to learn to spend time a new way—playing and relaxing instead of constant worry about survival.

It has been very rewarding to watch these two learn to trust, play and clown around, and relax into their housecat lives.

More than anything, living in the woods has taught me a great respect for Mother Nature. Without shelter or protection, humans can easily perish in winter conditions where I live. It's exponentially worse for a domesticated animal as small as a cat, without adequate shelter.

My heart goes out to these animals, and those people who do what they can to rescue, foster, adopt, or ensure that the animals don't suffer. We humans share a unique bond with animal companions, who can give us so much in return for the care we give them.

SEVERAL YEARS LATER, Kieran had become a very affectionate cat. He loved a lap. He'd offer his belly (not all cats will do this) and he loved his butt scratched. We'd sing to him as we scratched his hips, and we'd smile, watching him descend into bliss. His eyes would shut and his butt wiggled back and forth and he turned up the purr. Kieran played and loved to wrestle with the boy cats. He groomed the other cats and they groomed him. And he'd sit in the window forever, watching a feral cat roam the premises, or simply staring at the grass and the woods. Rehabilitation is possible and every cat has its own timetable.

Solstice is the time of transition. Winter solstice is the time when dark surrenders to light. Kieran's transition on winter solstice, was hopefully, one from dark to light.

Kieran, the Solstice cat.
(Photo courtesy of the author.)

Milo—A Shooting Star

O UR STREET-SMART CAT named Milo was adopted by us while Chris was finishing his Ph.D. thesis. Milo had been rescued by my cat-loving friend Lori, the same friend who helped me begin to appreciate cats. Lori lived in an apartment with pet restrictions. She had her allowed quota of two cats and was looking for a home for this fat-faced orange tom named Milo. Lori didn't have a lot of money, but she managed to get Milo neutered by a vet tech friend. Milo had almost been feral, so the fact that Lori was able to rescue him was an accomplishment itself. Her apartment complex was densely designed, with apartments in very close quarters, and Milo had been wandering the premises, howling. Lori had been afraid someone would hurt the cat to make him shut up.

We took Milo, and my memory of his appearance was that his big fat face dwarfed the rest of his too-thin body. Milo had the jowly cheeks of toms that have never been neutered, or have been neutered later in life (four years or after, according to one of my vets). He had orange (almost red) fur, tabby markings, and a dominant no-messing-around attitude. At the time, we had two other cats (Tigger and Jamie). Milo quickly handed Jamie his head. Chris witnessed the moment that Jamie was put in his place.

Jamie, of course, had been used to being boss. He lorded it over Tigger. When Milo came into the household, Jamie tried to one-up him. According to Chris, in the span of a few seconds, Milo smacked Jamie in the face and established dominance. No messing around, no frills, no posturing. Quick, dirty, and done.

Jamie and Milo became buddies after that, and would often play and cuddle together. I have many photos of these two very differ-ent orange cats hanging out together. Throughout Jamie's long life, the only cat he'd willingly snuggle with, or let groom him, was Milo.

Milo had been an outdoor stray and did not take to the indoors kindly. He wanted out on his terms, but we were not going to allow it for any of the cats. To voice his displeasure, Milo howled at the top of his lungs for the first three months in our house. Chris was under some stress of his own—his mother was dying of cancer on the east coast, and he was hurrying to finish his Ph.D. thesis. Milo's constant howling almost got him thrown out of the house. The upside of this, however, is that Milo and Chris established a strong bond that would last through Milo's life. Milo loved Chris and loved to be held by him and snuggle with him. Milo was less enamored with me. He liked me, possibly even loved me, but he would squirm if I tried to hold him.

I wrote a poem about about Milo and his loud voice, which was published in a poetry journal.

Trash Can Tom

Knocking over trash cans
scrounging for the last bit of food
that's Milo
loving, grudgeless orange tom
tipping cans
sardine breath
dig faster
no food around the corner
Where to sleep?
Aaaaooooowwwww!
A saxophone in a former life
howling the blues.

MILO'S HIND LEGS were always weaker than his front legs. We suspected he'd been hit by a car in his previous time as a stray, and a veterinary examination supported this. Milo made up for hind-end weakness with sturdy front legs and a huge muscular chest. The jowliness of his fat face gradually went away as he got older.

Chris often joked that our cats were "freeloaders," and it's true cats have a great life in our house. But Milo, Chris said, was the only cat that earned his keep. Milo not only inspired the "Trash Can Tom" poem, but he also inspired a very short book called *The Orange Cat Club*.

Occasionally, I go to the city to give my creative force a jolt. On a visit to San Francisco in 1998, I sat in a coffee shop and penned *The Orange Cat Club* in one sitting. The story starred Milo and featured a group of orange cats that bring the world to a peaceful and happier place with the example of their love. Here's an excerpt:

> "Let's form the Orange Cat Club,"
> the elder cats said,
> and drew on the vision
> to make the dream happen.
> There were cats far and wide
> of cinnamon color
> who pricked up their ears
> and took heed of the call.

The Orange Cat Club did well. I did not have the funds to produce it as a real book, but I photoshopped pictures and created a Publisher document. I sold 100-200 copies the first year. Milo certainly earned his keep at the "great, legendary cat house"—Chris's name for our place.

As Milo grew older, he mellowed. He began to let me hold him more, and he seemed to actually enjoy it. He'd stay in my arms for a long time, purring contentedly. He remained top cat in the household, and particularly enjoyed cuddling with Target.

Endings are inevitable, though they never get easier to accept. In the passing of an animal, I don't know whether a slow ending or a fast ending is better. Both have their advantages and disadvantages.

With a slow ending, you get lots of time to say goodbye, and the entire process can also be emotionally draining. With a fast ending, you have shock at something being torn so suddenly from your life. Milo's ending was somewhere in between, and as endings go—almost perfect, if such a word can be used. It was perfectly orchestrated. "Orchestrated" is a good word to use, for we were later to learn that Milo considered himself a "maestro" who kept things running smoothly.

At seventeen years, the only change we noticed was that Milo seemed to need to eat more and more. We fed him whatever he wished. He loved raw venison. Milo had always had an iron gut and could tolerate any kind of food.

On a wintertime Thursday, he weakened suddenly in his rear legs. By Saturday, he was howling and in pain. Local vets were closed, so we drove two hours to the closest emergency vet. The snow was flying, and we had to take two cars since Chris had to continue onto Wisconsin for a taxidermy course. I had Milo in my vehicle and he had stopped howling. I didn't know whether to be concerned or hopeful.

When we reached the emergency vet, we hurried in. I carried Milo in the plastic bottom of a cat carrier. He seemed too light. Where was the beefy, saucy street cat we'd spent our lives with? I stroked him and told him that I loved him, I scratched his checks—his face had gotten thinner as he got older.

As we waited in the lobby, a resident black cat came up to greet Chris. Target, Milo's buddy and our first and only black cat to that point, had passed four months ago to the date.

Chris petted the black cat and seemed comforted by his presence.

The vet ushered us into an exam room, told us to wait, and took Milo off to be examined. Then she reentered, with Milo. Milo kept his eyes fixed on us.

The vet told us that Milo had a thrombosis—a clot that had traveled down his spine and into his hips. He was paralyzed. She discovered a large tumor in his abdomen. I do not remember how I felt. I know I was glad not to be alone—that Chris and I could go through this together. The vet said with a lot of work and expense, Milo might be made better, but he would never have the same health that he once did. After she discovered the tumor, her countenance seemed even less encouraging.

"I do not say this lightly," said the vet, "but given all that is going on with your cat, I recommend euthanasia."

Chris and I hesitated. I felt immense tiredness drape itself over me like a heavy blanket. The room was bright and white—winter sun shone in one window at the season's odd angle. Milo lay on the steel counter in the plastic bottom of a cat carrier—watching us, communicating through those orange/green eyes. He winked at us once.

We nodded at the vet.

"Take the time you need," she said, "and knock on the door when you're ready." She disappeared into the adjoining surgical room, shutting the door behind her.

The nature of our relationship with Milo was long and multifaceted. That day, as we said goodbye to our orange and street-smart cat, we laughed and we cried. We stroked him and we thanked him. "Milo," said Chris in a tough-guy voice, "I knew you when you was a kitten." We thanked Milo for his verve, his moxie, his spirit. Milo held us with his eyes and winked at us once more.

We knocked on the door.

Milo and Jamie, enjoying life.
(Photo courtesy of the author.)

Milo, the loud orange tabby who was Chris's cat until the end.
(Photo courtesy of the author.)

Courage

A few days ago, I asked my husband to tell me when he'd seen me be most courageous. I thought he'd recall when I'd gone into business for myself, or struck out
on a new career, or stood up to a person and set some firm boundaries.

Instead, my husband recalled when we had to put Milo to sleep.

My husband's answer surprised me. I didn't think of Milo's euthanasia as a time
of courage. It happened so fast, and oddly, it seemed like the most natural thing
to do. Not that it was easy, but it was right. And we knew it. And sad as it was,
there was also a beauty in the experience.

What is courage? Is it, like my husband says, when you're backed into a corner
and you have to make the only (and most difficult) choice possible? Or is it when
we get out of our own way and act naturally, from the place of greatest integrity?
Milo's passing had that latter feeling to me.

I had to muster some courage when an eighteen-year-old cat of mine needed to
go under anesthesia to have a painful tooth removed. It gets very risky to anes-
thetize an older cat, but the alternative was that it was getting more painful for
the cat to eat. My cat still had a lot of will to live and a feisty spirit, all of which
played into my decision. I don't know that I did such a good job of getting out of
my own way—I stressed the entire time my cat was in surgery. My cat came
through surgery fine.

Here's to courage—knowing when we need it, knowing when to muster it.

It's All Good

If there was a phrase that summed up Milo's attitude toward life, it'd be something like, "It's all good." Milo had an easygoing, unflappable personality. Nothing bothered him and things rolled off his back. He was easy, and he was cool.

When Milo passed on, I often imagined he was saying those words to me from cat heaven. I'd talk to him when I walked down our road. "It's All Good" started to make me smile, whether I saw it on sweatshirts or on coffee mugs. We bought a coffee mug with the saying on it, and it sits on the top of our refrigerator, a constant reminder to me of the joy, love, and sometimes-heartache of having animal companions.

Milo sent me a shooting star the night of his death, and I knew that indeed, all was good. I had to bring him home after we had him put to sleep, a two-hour return trip from the emergency vet on a Sunday afternoon. I wanted time with his body before I had to let it go. At home, nighttime came and I knew I had to put him in the freezer—the ground was frozen so we could not bury him, and we had decided to cremate him with a local vet. Another step in the grieving process. I took Milo out to the garage, wrapped his body gently in a plastic bag, and set him temporarily in our chest freezer until I could take him to the local vet the next day for cremation.

Sighing, I turned from the freezer. More letting go. I stood in the garage doorway and looked out and up at a country night sky full of stars. Something released in me, and I looked at the sky and said, "thank you."

A shooting star dropped from the sky, in an absolutely vertical line, right in the center of my range of vision.

Sometime later, eighteen-year-old Jamie faced surgery for a very painful tooth. Anesthesia is risky for old cats. Jamie pulled through fine though I worried for the several hours while he was in surgery. When I went to pick him up and settle the bill at the vet's office, I also got instructions for mixing antibiotic for another cat in the household. The vet tech probably picked up on that I was having a tough time retaining the details.

She nodded. "Call us if you have any questions."

"I get so crazy when I go through this," I tried to explain.

She smiled. "It's all good," she said.

"I Love You" Is Universal

Put yourself in the frame of mind you're in when you're loving your cat, your dog, your child.

Then imagine living every moment of life in that frame of mind.

When I hold my orange cat Chester, I'm joyful. I smile with delight. I soften. I stroke his silky fur, admire his cute fat face, marvel at his long white whiskers, adore his paws, talk to him in nicknames, tell him how ecstatic I am that he is here. Chester picks up on this and leans into me, purring. My happiness quotient goes up . . . Up . . . UP.

I'm in love.

Imagine the possibilities if I lived in this frame of mind all the time.

I decided to try an experiment a few days ago and it has been interesting. I've been admiring and loving everything I come into contact with. I took a long walk and I really started to notice stuff. I admired the pattern of bare aspen branches against the sky. I told each tree I loved it. I loved the white pines and spruce and I told them that. I loved the crusty snow on the shoulder of the road. I loved the house I passed by, and the people in it, leading their lives. I was so busy loving, I didn't have any time for negative thoughts. What a concept! And yes, I worked on loving myself too. Sometimes that is the hardest jump for many of us. I thanked my body for health. I loved my strength and my ability to walk.

Still, what a practice, to walk around consciously loving things, people, nature, whatever came up in my path.

I figure, why not try to do more of this? I certainly spend enough time going the negative route. It is easy to get sucked into negative thinking. And it's a long-engrained habit. But yoga, and life, have taught me how to be aware of habits, and how to release the unhelpful habits, and establish new ones.

Think about your cat or animal companion and the pure love connection you feel between them and you. Then try feeling love and contentment as life passes by you. Insert love into your observations and your interactions. There's a huge potential for transformation in many forms with this simple action.

The Courtship of Karma and the Courtship of Two Day

KARMA AND TWO DAY were cats that looked as if they could be related. Both had beautiful silver tabby markings, and Karma also had a brush of brown Siamese. Both had blue eyes, though Karma's were larger and brighter. Two Day's eyes were smaller than Karma's, and closer together.

Both Karma and Two Day were strays that showed up near our house. But these two cats never courted each other. Rather, we courted each cat, more than a decade apart, to tempt them inside so they'd not perish in our cold northern Minnesota winters.

Karma showed up in 1998. Two Day showed up in the winter of 2010 and came back, pre-winter 2011. I always worried when cats showed up pre-winter. I sensed their desperation. They needed a warm place to stay. I was not always sure I had the room.

When Karma showed up, we already had three cats in the house, and I didn't think there was room to add another. In November, the weather was starting to turn cold and bitter. Snow would be here soon. I can't remember when we first noticed the very small grayish cat with incredible markings on its front legs. It was skittish and we could not get too close to it. For some reason, I assumed it was a boy, although we learned differently later.

Sometimes, I saw the cat running scared in the tall grass. (There was a time when we mowed less of our lawn, before we became aware of fire danger and before we'd endured a few winters with little snow when the tall grass did not get mashed down.) The wind whipped the grass around and made the spruce and aspen sing with warnings of winter. The cat ran back and forth, looking scared and confused about where to go. She didn't leave the yard. It was as if she didn't want to approach the house, but was frightened to wander off farther.

The small gray cat courted us—or at least that was the story we told ourselves. Visible from our south-facing French doors was the entrance to a mowed path, which led from the yard to our field in back of the property. The cat would sit at the opening of the path, with her back to the house, staring into the distance. She may have been hunting. She may have been daydreaming. We saw her do this many times, and we joked that she was being coy.

I decided to try and tempt her closer to the house, slowly.

I set out food in a dish, far from the house and at the entrance to the path. She ate greedily. Over a period of days, I moved the dish closer to the house. She didn't resist. Eventually the cat was eating so close to the house she was practically in the front doorway.

I took the next step and brought the food dish right inside the door. I knew she was close by. I propped the door open and I waited. Would the gray, silver, and brownish cat dare to enter the house?

I must have gotten distracted because when I checked next, the cat had come in through the door and had finished all the food. I didn't want her to leave and I couldn't get around her to close the door. Grabbing the nearest thing I could find, a Dixie cup, I filled the cup with more food and set it down in front of her.

She ate greedily, and got her head stuck in the cup. I have an eternal memory of a small gray cat in our breezeway, cup stuffed over her head, swiveling her head back and forth.

I shut the door.

The cup fell off her head and she ran the only way she could— into the house. She went into the first hiding place she could find, our tiny laundry/utility room off to the right. I let her be by herself to settle down.

Gradually, I dared reach a hand into the utility room. She was curled up on a white dust mop, back against the water heater. She did not run when I petted her. She purred, and rubbed my hand, and purred some more. Quite soon after, she climbed into my lap.

KARMA TURNED OUT to be a gem of a cat. Not only was she a stunner in the looks department (picture an amazing mix of tabby legs and face, Siamese-colored torso, huge blue eyes, and a tiny black tail with almost invisible stripes) but she had a nurturing, sweet personality. She got along with everyone, human and animal, in the household. She loved to play and she loved attention. She learned to stand on her hind legs on a dining chair, with front paws against the headboard of the chair. This was her way to say, "look at me, pet me, I am adorable." She loved the boy cats, and Karma and one of the boys often cuddled and groomed each other.

But Karma never showed an interest in going outside. When she did slip outside once, it was fortunate we were close and able to grab her. Once outside, she instantly became distant, scared and almost feral. It was almost as if another personality took over.

We brought her inside and Chris held her. At one point he took her into the bedroom and showed her the window. "Look," he said. "You're inside. You're safe."

She shrank from the window and buried her head in Chris's chest, and didn't relax until we took her away from the window and back into the center of the house.

Scream Like a Cat

Several years ago, a well-known life coach challenged me to speak out and use my voice.

Patrick Ryan made me embody a cat. In a weekend of already intense training to become a life coach, Patrick pushed me to act out the part of a cat, purr like a cat, crawl like a cat, and scream like a cat. All in front of thirty classmates, seated in a circle around me.

This was a real leap. I'm not a screamer. I'm quiet and not comfortable drawing attention to myself. But where Patrick was going went beyond whether a person is boisterous or quiet. With his uncanny talent as a life coach, Patrick sensed that I was holding back in life. I was not truly and fully using my "Voice." I was not truly and fully expressing the truth of who I am.

How many of us go through life like this? Sacred to step into who we are. Afraid to be completely and truly ourselves. Holding back. Being safe. Not risking. I've been there many times. I am still there. And I have to admit, although I screamed like a cat for Patrick, I still held back. I could have screamed louder. I could have turned myself inside out. I could have leapt completely, not halfway.

Patrick taught me something that will stay with me forever, and I am beginning to grasp its enormity.

Your cats don't hold back. They scream, whine, emote, demand, yowl, purr, love. They are completely and fully themselves as cats. Whether you're a cat, an artist, an activist, a whatever—be it. Love fully. Live in compassion. Don't be afraid to completely love your cats, or to completely face the fact that eventually they will depart. Give your heart to everything. Our animal companions are amazing teachers of love. Live in the moment and enjoy it. And be yourself. It is the truest and best path to a happy and phenomenal life.

TWO DAY, ON THE OTHER HAND, was probably feral. I cannot say for sure.

October 2011 was an unseasonably warm fall following a dangerously dry summer. A huge forest fire burned thousands of acres in the nearby Boundary Waters Canoe Area wilderness.

The warmth was working in Two Day's favor, but we knew that the weather would turn soon. We had some cold nights and on those days, when the air got dryer and had that suggestion of a cold bite, I sensed that Two Day got a little more desperate, just by watching the way that he acted. A cynic would say that Two Day was playing me, but I preferred to give him the benefit of the doubt.

I had five cats inside now and I didn't think it would be a good idea to take another. Still, I worried about this guy.

Two Day first showed up in 2010, pre-winter. Our neighbor, who lived four miles down the road from us (it's a rural area and sparsely populated) had a cat hanging around that he called Two Day—since the cat would show up every two days or so. The neighbor described this cat as a Siamese-looking cat—probably a boy. So when this cat showed up here, we figured it might be Two Day, even though this guy looked more like a gray tabby. The name stuck.

Pre-winter 2010, we fed Two Day, gradually bringing the food closer to the house. Eventually we put the food in the garage. I had no hopes of getting Two Day in the house, but I hoped to train him to use the garage in the winter. At least it would be some shelter from the cold. We watched him come in and out of the garage and our plan seemed to be working. We had straw for the chicken coop toward the back of the garage, and we had piles of old sheets and blankets in back that we used for covering the garden when frost threatened. I had a feeling the cat was bedding down at night, hopefully getting some warmth from these blankets or straw.

Once a year in November, deer hunters from all over the state descended upon our woods. Our property abutted state land that hunters loved to use. Hunting season had opened and I worried about

Two Day. It wasn't as if I was able to grab this feral cat and get him inside.

A band of about five men, dressed in orange and somewhat noisy, walked down our dirt road to head into the state land area. I saw Two Day run into the woods, unfortunately in the same direction the men were headed.

We did not see Two Day again, that fall or winter. We wondered, with a bit of worry, whether he'd been shot, or had frozen to death.

THE YEAR 2011 BROUGHT lots of traveling for me as I promoted my book and took a bit of yoga training during Jamie's illness. Chris and I kept in touch through phone calls and emails.

One email from Chris ended like this:

"BTW, Two Day showed up. He's eating like a horse!"

Two Day had come back! It was nice news that counterbalanced all the worrying I was doing about Jamie.

Two Day hung around in the summer of 2011. We had no idea how he survived the 2010 winter, which was colder than usual. As winter approached again, I had no solution for integrating Two Day, as the house was full with five cats.

The office was a possibility, although I doubted I could get him in there. Two Day had the conflicted personality of a cat who was part-feral and part-domesticated. I remember looking out the western window of the house at one point, which faced the entrance to my office (separate from the house). There stood Two Day making a show of rubbing the office door, as if he was saying "This is mine. I would like to go in here." However, I was not sure I could actually tempt him into the office. He continued to let us feed him and he slept in the garage, enjoying the remaining autumn warmth.

Contentment

I give yoga a lot of credit for how abundant and happy I've felt lately.

For me, yoga is more than stretching. It's a way of life. And practicing yoga has taught me to be truly, authentically content with even the smallest things. I think it's because yoga helps me be in the moment. That's an overused phrase, but it is true. When I am focusing on what I'm doing in the present, and not racing around worrying about the future, or the past, I enjoy things a lot more. Including my time with my cats.

I've brushed Chester daily for the last four days. I really love doing this and he really really loves it. Some cats adore being brushed—Chester is one. I simply focus on what I'm doing and enjoy each second. I also enjoy his reactions. He closes his eyes, purrs, butts up against the brush, and makes it clear he wants more.

Then I brush whoever else will tolerate it. I stay in the moment and enjoy it. It's such a simple thing to stay in the moment, to just breathe and slow down, and it does make life much more fun.

I watch the cats play. This is enormous fun. Sometimes, I join in. They have a lot to teach me about letting go of work for a few moments so I can throw the "baba"—Chester's favorite stuffed catnip pillow toy (he chases it and will fetch it). Or, I stop working when I hear them playing with their newest favorite toy, a circular track with a sparkling ball (twenty-one dollars at a local Petco). Inside the circle is a rough cardboard scratching area. They love this toy. All of them. And it makes me happy to watch them having so much fun.

Does this hurt my productivity as a freelancer who works from home? I don't think so. I think I'm more productive with the fun little breaks. I go back to work and am more alert, and work faster. Timeouts to enjoy life (including my cats) are just as beneficial as time for workouts, yoga, or to take a walk. And I think it's a great survival skill. If I can be content with my circumstances, then I have less of those nagging and anxious feelings of "I need more," "I don't have enough," etc.

It's a great thing.

Attachment

HOW DO YOU AVOID getting attached to a cat?

How do people have outdoor cats without getting attached?

These are the questions that Two Day inspired.

We watched this feral cat come and go at our house, and increasingly come. He walked in for food, heading to his dish right inside the garage door. Generally he showed no fear. He seemed to like to listen to me talk.

"Two Day!" I called out. "You're such a handsome boy!"

He listened, and he followed me with his eyes. Chris was convinced Two Day waited for me. When I wasn't home—for example, traveling for some book-related business—Chris swore Two Day was waiting and looking for me.

And for me, it got to the point that the household felt incomplete if Two Day was not hanging around.

He was an outdoor cat, and I worried when he didn't show up for more than a day, though it only happened occasionally.

Of course, this led me to think of the yoga tenet non-possessiveness (or nonattachment). Once I form bonds with something, someone, or some idea, I get more wrapped up in it. I find it harder to let go. The mind whirls.

But as the time went on, and we headed into November, it seemed Two Day was making it increasingly easier for me to get attached. He wouldn't let me touch him yet, but he was hanging closer and closer to the house. In fact, he hardly wandered out of sight. He seemed content to bed down in the garage—either on straw on the floor, or in a makeshift bed of blankets in a large rubber container. He sat near the house as if it was his own—next to the garage door, by the picnic table on the deck, or against the west side of the house,

Adaptability

My cat, Karma, is wearing an Elizabethan collar for the next several days. The collar goes around a cat or dog's neck and prevents them from scratching or irritating a part of their body that may need to heal for some reason. Milo, for example, had to wear the collar once when he got a wound on his ear which he made worse and wouldn't leave alone. The collar prevented him from biting and licking the wound, and allowed the wound to heal.

Karma, for reasons yet unknown, suddenly started overly grooming her legs. Because cats have a barbed tongue, they can lick an area raw with enough effort. Soon, the hair was missing on the inside of Karma's legs. The vet ruled out any obvious skin disorders and suggested the collar to make sure the hair would grow back and the skin would heal. Sometimes cats and dogs do this for psychological reasons. Our vet suspected a food allergy in Karma's case.

The interesting thing about Karma's collar-wearing experience has been how well she's adapted to this clumsy contraption around her neck. At first she was distressed—backing up, going forward, moving erratically. I was worried she'd bump up against the hot walls of our woodstove. But Karma adapted quickly. She eats, drinks, and goes to the bathroom, regardless of the collar. She's walking well with it on, even jumping. She's learned to thrust her head under Chester's face for a grooming, and he grooms her face, regardless of the cone. It didn't take her long to adjust to a "new normal."

We're able to start to take the collar off, now, as her legs are looking better. But I'm encouraged by how easily she adapted to something which seemed to really unnerve her at first. It speaks of the ability of all of us, all species, to adapt when we need to.

watching me work in the office, seeing my head through the office window. He acted like he wanted to come in, but he only flirted with the idea. Perhaps it was simply that he knew food was near, and he didn't want to stray too far.

MY HEART WAS BROKEN by Two Day. I was played by a feral cat!

Things were going smoothly. Too smoothly. Two Day was hanging around. I'd pull into the driveway and he'd be snuggled into the corner garden that bordered the right side of the garage door. He'd meow at the shop door in the morning. He walked into the shop several times, and looked around. We didn't force him to stay. He curled up on the porch, and soaked in the rare heat off the side of the house. We didn't have snow on the ground yet; it was November 5, but very nice and very unusual for that time of year.

But it had been very cold at night.

Two Day had gotten into the habit of spending a lot of time in the garage. He seemed to be quite comfortable. Many days, he'd sleep in the garage all day. I was worried that something was wrong with him. I had noticed a raw place at the base of one of his ears that looked like an injury, or a place he couldn't leave alone.

I knew this particular night would be quite cold (ten degrees or possibly a little lower). Friends that have more knowledge of outdoor cats than I do had reassured me that cats would do just fine in this weather as long as they had shelter around them. Still, I worried. I knew the garage would be really draft free if I just shut the door all the way. It was a new garage door, and Chris had recently plugged all the leaks in the garage with caulking and insulation. Two Day was lying in his straw bed for the night. I put out food, and figured he'd be okay until the morning.

I closed the garage door all the way, instead of leaving it the customary one or two feet up from the floor.

The next morning, I was up at 5:30 a.m. as usual. I went to the shop and opened the door to the garage. Two Day stood at the door, meowing. I opened the garage door.

He left, ignoring the food. He never returned. Gone! Played by a feral! I hope. I hoped he played me and was still alive, charming someone else into feeding him and giving him a soft bed in a garage or a barn. I missed his entertainment and the relationship we were starting to build. I missed the way he stood on the top of the roof peak of our sauna, staring intently at the ground for hours, hunting. I missed how he jumped the one precious time I was able touch him (I touched my finger to his head as he ate). I missed pulling into the driveway and seeing him relaxing outside, near the house, in a garden, or against the wall.

I hoped he was well.

Kali's Story

AMONG MY CATS lives a three-legged cat named Kali. At the time I first met Kali, I volunteered at the regional Humane Society. Why would a person like me, a person who already has a houseful of cats, volunteer at the Humane Society?

Good question. I think of those cats there, and the love they need. I have to realize I can't save the world, or every cat. But I have gone off topic.

Kali stared at me from a cage in the Humane Society. She had brilliant green eyes and tabby markings—a black-and-silver-striped coat with a beautiful golden undercoat. A white bib and off-center white markings on her nose completed the picture. She had gold rims around her eyes. She was a a beautiful cat, yet despite that, I didn't notice her right away.

I had lost Tigger recently. During Tigger's ten-year life, she lost a rear leg to cancer. Kali had a rear leg missing, as well. A woman I know who probably places too much importance on signs and omens (even more than I do) told me this was a sign. I acted on the sign and adopted Kali.

IN JUNE 1999, my first cat Tigger died from an aggressive cancer, which was the result of a sarcoma (tumor) that had metastasized from a vaccination site. Tigger's cancer treatment had included the amputation of one rear leg to try and stave off the advancing malignancy.

In July I went to the local Humane Society to be with the animals. I was not ready to adopt but I was grieving deeply and needed the comfort of being around cats.

Maybe a part of me hoped I'd find Tigger again. What I did find was another three-legged cat.

"Misty," as the Humane Society had named her, had been abandoned in an apartment by a tenant in trouble with the law. According to the landlord, sometime in this cat's past, a child had put a rubber band on the cat's rear leg and had forgotten to take it off. The leg had to be amputated. Misty was small. One friend later called her a salt-and-pepper cat. She had brown, black, white, and gray in her tabby coat.

I took Misty into a room at the shelter and played with her. She was lively and liked the attention. I left. We already had two male cats and one female. The last thing I needed was one more cat in a small house, especially since the three at home got along well. I worried I would upset the balance if I added another.

My friend prodded me, intrigued that another three-legged cat had shown up in my life. "There must be a reason for this. Maybe you're meant to have this cat."

I went back and adopted her. I told Tigger's story to a staff person, hoping she didn't see the tears that were growing in my eyes.

The transition was rocky, as Misty brooked no nonsense and refused to submit to the male cats. She would rush right into the middle of Milo and Jamie's playing, and would growl and break it up like a referee. A friend told us that Misty reminded her of the fierce, yet compassionate, Hindu goddess Kali Ma. The new name stuck.

Kali loved a human lap and climbed up instantly whenever we sat down. Slowly, she seemed to become more secure in our home. I told her repeatedly this was her home for good. Like Tigger, Kali Ma did extremely well on three legs. She could really move fast when she wanted to, and could run around just as fast as any of the other cats.

Several months later, acquaintances stopped by to see an electrical system we'd installed. The woman sat on the floor, playing with Kali.

She looked up. Her expression was hard to read.

"This is Mitzi," she said emphatically, pointing to the cat.

The story came out in pieces; how a family member had accidentally put a bootie on the cat's leg and forgotten to take it off; how the child saved the money to have her leg amputated rather than having her put down; how they'd later given the cat to another home. I remember the look on the woman's face as she held Kali for a long time. I remember Kali's acceptance of the woman. Later, I told one of the animal control officers at the Humane Society the rest of the story.

"Yep," she said softly, "the animals don't hold any grudges, do they?"

We were both crying.

Noticing the Less Noticed

I've recently made it a practice to better appreciate where I live.

We live in the boreal forest of the northern Midwest U.S. Our area is low with wetlands and swamps, and very little topography. The woods have been logged and what used to be pure boreal forest is transitioning, due to logging and climate change, to more of a deciduous aspen forest. My engrained prejudice is that aspen is not a particularly stunning tree.

There are spruce as well, some of them quite old. Most are black spruce, not as showy as Colorado blue spruce or some of the other spruces. I love the stark and prehistoric outline that these spruce make against a sky uninterrupted with buildings. And there are tamaracks, which grow in lowlands and which I have always liked. The tamaracks turn gold in the fall before they drop their needles. These trees have been brilliant this year—the brightest I have ever seen. There are a few birches, and lots of scrubby alder (another swamp tree). Because of the way this forest grows, it can be difficult or impossible to walk through. It doesn't have the primordial feel of a New England forest or of the California redwoods.

Our forest has been taken from. It's been logged. People hunt it heavily for deer and grouse. People generally don't wax romantic about this swampy woods, though they might be more enthused about nearby lakes. Minnesota is blessed with an abundance of water resources.

I had an "Aha" moment recently. This forest needs to be appreciated rather than just being taken from. So I have made it a practice to tell my forest how much I appreciate and love it. I study the beauty of bare and intricate aspen branches against a gray fall sky. I walk through a thin carpet of golden tamarack needles on my driveway, and thank the brilliant larch trees that dropped those needles. I look at and I find love for the dry sedge grass, the Labrador tea plant, the other swamp plants, and the old spruce that seem to be draped with a light green moss. It's all just as surreal and beautiful as the redwoods or the New England maples. And I want to keep telling it so because it seems to drink it up. It needs to be loved.

I also do the same thing in my household of cats. Six cats keep a person busy. Sometimes, someone falls to the bottom of the pile. I'd say most often, that's been my cat Kali, a super-sweet three-legged cat who was abandoned earlier in life. Yet she loves every human she's ever met, even though I wouldn't blame her if she shunned us all. Kali is sweet, sturdy, and strong. When a respiratory virus made my cats ill last winter, it didn't touch Kali.

Kali never complains, has needed less care than the other cats, and isn't as vocal about getting her attention or her needs met. It's easy to miss her. And that's something I need to change. I will be practicing loving and giving back to all my cats, just as I am learning to love and give back to my forest.

Watching, Wanting, Waiting

JAMIE WATCHED ME TODAY, through the glass doors that lead out to our deck. I was beyond the deck and in the garden, thirty to forty feet from the window that Jamie sat behind. With his one eye, he watched me intently.

I was thrilled.

Daily, I asked myself—was I crazy? In denial? Optimist, or afraid to face the truth? Was I reading too much into every mannerism that seemed to indicate Jamie was still with it, and engaged in life?

He watched me as I pulled weeds in blazing heat. I didn't want to let him outside yet. It was too hot for a cat whose main hydration was through a needle under the skin. It was too hot for any animal. I was only out in it because it was summer and I spent as much time outside as I could. When winter came, there would be plenty of time to be inside.

I was thrilled.

I thought it was great that Jamie could focus on me at such a distance. I thought to myself, *he looks good.* His eye had fire and interest. The vets told me I'd know when it was time. "You'll see it in his eyes," they said. I hadn't seen it in his eye yet. In fact, he seemed to be getting stronger. The high calorie food was kicking in. The Lactated Ringer's solution was at the maximum dose. I'd gotten very good at pricking him under the skin, and he was tolerating it.

To the uninitiated, Jamie would look scary. He was an old, very thin cat, with hair missing on his legs and around his face. We didn't know why the hair was missing. His tongue was not working but he still tried to groom himself after he ate. All I could guess was that the action of rubbing his nose against his legs caused the hair to go away. That action said to me that Jamie was still interested in living.

And as long as he was still interested in living, I was going to do my best to keep him alive.

There were days I doubted myself and wondered if this task was too much, even for me. It was demanding and the food and the Lactated Ringer's solution could not be missed. Still, this time taught me a lot about contentment—my own contentment. I was extremely content when Jamie purred, when he groomed himself, when he rode shoulders, when he showed the desire to go outside, when he was interested in food even though he couldn't eat by himself, when he climbed up on the bed to snuggle close to my head. I couldn't believe I was such an optimist—it showed me a new side of myself. I was finding good in everything Jamie did and he was teaching me a lot.

It seems at this time, when animals approach the end of their lives, that these companions become more than animals. They become teachers with powerful lessons. I believe animals are teachers all their lives—but the lessons become painfully and readily apparent at this unique, charged time.

Jamie showed me I was more of an optimist than I realized. I'd do anything to coax a purr out of him. Even the other cats were dealing well with the decreased attention they were getting.

Chris said there were no rights or wrongs in this situation. We had to trust we were doing the best we could, that Jamie was not suffering, and that he still had a quality of life. We believed Jamie was still enjoying life. But it was difficult. It brought up my own mortality of course, and it also let every fear and resentment I had about loss—any kind of loss—come right up to the surface. I was grieving that I had no community. Of course that was not true: I had friends, I had students, I had professional peers, I had a wonderful husband, I had loving animals. I had a family I care about. But going through grief can distort the rest of life. I was tired.

At these times, I looked to the animals. They had lots of lessons for me about contentment, strong will, living in the moment, and unrestrained, unconditional love.

The Reluctant Mouser

True story:

Rama (black cat) stares at a bi-fold door on the floor. The door has been taken down from its frame temporarily so the dryer could be pulled out of the laundry closet and repaired.

Rama sits, and stares, and stares, for hours and hours. He's a patient mouser, and there's something under that door.

Something is under that door.

Rama waits and waits. He waits all day.

Momma cat (i.e., head cat, i.e., me) takes out pellets for a snack. The other four cats quickly come running, and have a few kibble-pellets off the floor.

Uncharacteristically, Rama ignores pellet sounds and the smell of food, and stares at the bi-fold door. He'll wait all night until that mouse comes out. Then, when it comes out, he'll get it. He's amazingly fast for a big cat. He'll play with the mouse and slowly kill it, as cats often do. Unless I rescue it.

Finally, hours later, husband picks up the door to reinstall. Mouse darts out. Rama grabs it.

Rama makes a big production, carrying mouse around and growling and acting proud. Then Rama releases mouse. Mouse is unharmed.

Mouse looks at Rama, and mouse stands still. Is mouse offering his life, or simply smart enough to know not to move?

Rama looks confused.

Rama grabs mouse again, tosses it around, acts proud, and lets mouse go.

Again, mouse stands right in front of Rama, not moving.

Rama looks confused. This is too easy!

Husband takes pity on mouse, grabs it (mouse lets him), and puts mouse outside in the garage.

???

Conclusion (?)—we are feeding Rama *way* too well, *or* the mouse wanted to die . . . or . . . the mouse was very smart and threw Rama a curve ball.

Silly cats.

Mukunda and Jamie

UKUNDA," I SAID to the cat on my lap. "What is grief?"

Maybe I thought it, instead of speaking aloud. It was late at night, and I was in a retreat center in the hills of northern California. In these mountains, I felt as if I walked between two worlds, and I was not sure what was real and unreal.

This burnished brown-and-orange cat stared at me. It was almost 10:00 p.m. in the Sierras of northern California. Strange things lurked in the woods, but I was on sacred ground. At this retreat center and yoga ashram, in a gentle yoga tradition founded by Paramahansa Yogananda that I'm not completely sure I buy, this magic cat had come into my lap during what may have been my own orange cat's last days of life.

My own orange cat, Jamie, was 1,900 miles away. My heart was torn and broken with grief. Jamie was at least twenty years old. My husband was giving Jamie the best of care so that I could be at this yoga course and retreat center. I was learning about how to heal people with yoga therapy, but Jamie might be leaving this world.

Mukunda sat in my lap.

Most people here had gone to bed. I was staying in a comfortable and basic building, and sharing a room with my friend and fellow yoga teacher, Wende. We had made plans months ago to come out here and to take this yoga therapy training for yoga teachers. One week before we were to depart, the mass under Jamie's tongue was discovered. It took every ounce of strength in me to not cancel my trip. I had to trust—leap off a cliff like the cliffs I had been leaping off lately—and visualize and hope that all would go well at home.

Now I sat in the foyer of the building where I was living for a week. And this magic cat, named with Paramahansa Yogananda's childhood name, snuggled into my lap.

This retreat center, or ashram, was part of an intentional spiritual community called Ananda. Ananda is based on the teachings of the Indian guru Paramahansa Yogananda. Yogananda was called "Mukunda" as a child. This cat, which has been adopted by the community, was said to be very insightful.

According to community members, it was a big deal when Mukunda sought you out. Mukunda didn't come to everyone. He'd walk right by, and sometimes, completely ignore all the people calling out to him. At the retreat center/ashram, there was a beautiful outdoor eating area. Mukunda would walk through, paying no attention to anyone. So I took notice, tonight, that he'd come to me. Even though I wasn't quite sure about this particular yoga tradition—something about it felt too sweet, too happy—I was open to anything and I appreciated the company.

I stroked Mukunda, trying to imagine he was Jamie. But Mukunda was nothing like Jamie. Mukunda was angular and sturdy at the same time. He had a hole through his ear that made me wince every time I looked at it. Mukunda's fur was smooth and coarse and short. Jamie was medium-haired, and had always had fine fur. Jamie had large, startled-looking eyes that gave his face a more innocent look than Mukunda's.

Mukunda sat in my lap and purred. He sat there for at least twenty minutes. I'd been heading out of my room to return two tea mugs to the kitchen. When I saw him waiting in the breezeway, I sat down. He climbed into my lap, purring, rubbing into me, kneading with his paws, even drooling.

This cat had healed me before. The previous year, I came to yoga training at this same ashram. The training (more yoga therapy) was exceptional, but the dynamic between me and another person in our group was difficult. I struggled with my feelings about this discordance, in a place that is an experiment in joyful living. At one point, when I was experiencing particular sorrow and emotion about the situation, Mukunda came to me. He let me hold him, and he purred his loud, rumbling "Ommm." We sat that way for several minutes. As I put him down, the woman who I had the difficult dynamic with appeared. She apologized for her behavior when we worked together. I think Mukunda made that moment of enlightenment possible for both of us.

What was Mukunda trying to teach me now? Why was he sitting in my lap, as my cat 1,900 miles away struggled with an oral tumor, and kept his will to live through it all? When did I have to step in, or did I? Could I miraculously heal and dissolve the tumor, through prayer and by tapping into the energy of this place? I had been trying.

I was unnerved and touched at the same time.

Can spiritual masters live through our animals? My animals have always been some of my greatest teachers. What was Mukunda trying to teach me? Was Yogananda in the presence of this cat, and did he have lessons for me—a person who liked this gentle tradition and this lovely place, but had no intention of joining this path?

Mukunda finally got off my lap—he saw something outside in the dark and began to stalk it. I went to bed, gently entering my room in the dark so I didn't wake Wende. But I didn't fall asleep until 1:00 a.m. At one point, coyotes burst into howling and yipping. I worried about Mukunda, but he had survived for a long time here in the Sierra foothills. As I tossed in my twin bed, I felt the edge of a credit-card sized piece of paper—my phone calling card. A sign to call home? Was Mukunda dead? Had Jamie passed on? I did not call home, but got a message the next morning that all was well. Jamie was maintaining.

Listen to the quiet voice of intuition, our teachers tell us. Then you will know it's intuition, and not ego. I hoped Jamie would clearly let us know what to do, in the minutes, days, hours, and time ahead.

Old Stories, New Stories

It seems I am getting more and more aware of my "old stories" lately. Yoga has a lot to do with helping me become aware of these stories. Somehow, when I get quiet and notice the patterns my mind takes, and get completely honest with myself—I become more aware of my old stories. Ultimately it is quite freeing.

What's an old story? Here's one I discovered myself doing yesterday. I have an old story that "it's very hard to be a writer." This surfaced for me when I learned that my first book would be published. Immediately, my mind created all kinds of stuff to go along with that: "I worked so hard for this," "I worked years for this," "No one will have any idea how special this is," "No one knows how hard it is to get published," blah . . . blah . . . blah.

Of course, some of this is true. It is hard to be a writer. It is hard to get published. It can take years and years and years. And many people don't have a clue about the process. But the freeing thing about becoming aware of my old stories is that I can recognize them and put them in their proper place. I don't have to expend mental energy regurgitating all this stuff, because none of it matters. Yes, it's hard to be a writer, but who cares? I'd write anyway. It's gone, and all the angst along with it. I'll still write, whether the old stories are in my head or not, so why not drop them? I find this really neat.

Do I have old stories about my cats? Not really. They're too pure, or different, or not neurotic enough, to inspire this kind of thinking in me. We can argue that cats are neurotic, and maybe they are. But somehow, they don't lead me to the kind of angst my old stories are capable of. And that's just another one of the gifts my cats give me—they help me keep my head on straight.

Mukunda, curious about the birdbath.
(Photo courtesy of the author.)

Act III:
Jamie—The Long Stretch to the End of the Road

*A*FTER MY JULY TRIP to upstate New York for my book reading and signing, I stayed home with no plans to go anywhere. I spent all my time with Jamie. Our moments grew more tender and deep. My heart was on an edge difficult to explain. I felt soft and vulnerable, vacillating between sorrow and joy. My understanding of love was more multifaceted than it had ever been—painful, sweet, tender, vulnerable, heavy, sad, and beyond understanding. I was surprised at my capacity to love.

Jamie knew something was happening. What was a cat's experience of this process? I have always been fascinated with what our animal companions seem to know. There is more to the human/animal companion bond than our language is capable of capturing. There are subtle gifts for us when we are ready.

When I reach the end of my life, I hope to say to myself, "I am glad I had the awareness to receive these gifts. I am glad I had the ability to carve out relationships with my animal companions that are more than I thought possible."

Jamie watched me. He wanted Chris and me in his sight at all times. He wanted to be with us, and he wanted us to be with him. We did the best we could and honored Jamie's wishes. Every moment was intense and full of possibilities.

In my yoga teacher training, our instructors talked about how a yoga practice, or any spiritual practice, can polish and refine you to the truest, best person you can be. Jamie was polishing us. We were becoming the best we could be. Love, sadness, and heartache surrounded our already golden house. The logs had been treated a year prior, and made the house glow. Love overrode it all. I was learning I was better than I realized. Chris was learning about the depth of his love. I was watching my husband's heart crack open.

I had a good friend, an artist, who died several years prior. She had cancer and chose to pass at home with minimum medical intervention. My friend, and her hospice worker, referred to this period of time as the long stretch. I realized then that death is a process, not a concrete occurrence that happens all at once. Death is a stretching. A twine exists between you and the other being. It seems it could stretch to infinity. Perhaps it does. Perhaps the quality of the twine simply changes when the being passes on from this world. I'd like to think the twine never breaks.

Jamie was getting ready to say goodbye. The twine was stretching. Chris and I went about our lives as best we could but we were ever aware of the twine, the stretching, the intensity of each moment. Adrenaline and sheer will kept us functioning. Often, I fell into a dead sleep, emotional exhaustion overcoming me. When I woke, I was startled all over, again and again, re-remembering what was happening in the house and what we were going through.

At the beginning of August, Jamie started to limp, favoring one front leg. The leg seemed weak. At first we wondered if he sprained it. Up until that point, Jamie had still been able to get on the couch or on the bed. We surmised that maybe he landed wrong on the floor.

But in the fast matter of a day or two, it became apparent he was losing the ability to walk. He could no longer hold himself up. He had the strength in his paws to grab things, or to get our attention, but he couldn't get anywhere. Suddenly, things got even more complicated. Jamie could no longer get to the bathroom on his own.

We held Jamie over the litter box to help him pee and poop. Amazingly, he did so. I continued to be impressed with how smart this cat was. But I am a movement person, a person who loves to do yoga and dance and walk and ski—and this new development jolted me. I wondered if this was it. How horrible it would be to not be able to walk. Did we need to make the decision and take this into our hands?

But Jamie was still alive, and interested. He still wanted to be near us. He head butted us and talked. As he lost the ability to move around, he became more vocal to get our attention. These were not cries of pain. They were deliberate noises and vocalizations to engage us and to get us to be close to him, touch him, or talk to him.

I couldn't believe this cat's will. He made every attempt to round out and deepen our relationship. If only I could live so well! If only I could remember how to make the most of each moment. Life was a huge gift, and Jamie knew it.

We made a platform Jamie could lay on, by taking a cardboard box and trimming down the sides to a two-inch height. We protected the box with plastic and towels. If Jamie had an accident, I washed him in the sink so he didn't smell. He could move, but he couldn't hold himself up. Letting go, I realized, was harder for me than I ever thought possible. What would I do when I had to lose people? My husband, if it happened? How could I handle this again?

"It's time," I told Chris.

It was a Friday.

Chris wasn't sure. But I couldn't bear the thought of my cat not being able to get around, not able to go to the bathroom on his own. I didn't mind doing the extra work of keeping him clean. It was just one more addition with all the other care-giving tasks we were already doing.

Horribly, reluctantly, I called the vet. I made an appointment for a Monday euthanasia. The clichés were true. It was the worst call in the world. Again, I had the deep sick feeling in my gut; again I was lightheaded. I was normally so sturdy, so tough. This was the thing that would take me down, this grief. I felt as if I was playing God. I felt as if I was letting Jamie down.

JAMIE WANTED TO LIVE. He didn't want to leave. Something was happening in his body. But his mind, his strong-willed mind, was another story. It didn't surprise me, and it did. In a strange way, it gave me joy.

Chris and I watched Jamie, and spent every minute possible with him, over the weekend.

OUR TIME WITH JAMIE reminded me of when my dad was passing on. Dad had muscular dystrophy, and it had eventually traveled to his swallowing muscles, as it does. This disease wastes all the muscles, though we tend to think of the more apparent muscles—the hamstrings, the calves, the biceps, first. Unless we are medical people or anatomists, we forget about the internal functioning muscles.

Dad had aspirated food or liquid, ending up in the hospital with pneumonia. He was on a respirator for two weeks, but Dad had a living will. Ethically, the hospital could not keep him on life support. The life support was removed on a Wednesday. The next day, Dad started to die. But something in him wasn't ready. He came back. Perhaps he still had goodbyes to say to friends. Perhaps his mind still had to get right with the fact that the body was shutting down. On Friday, we watched him, alert, sit up. He ate ice cream. He met once more with one of his dearest friends. Perhaps he needed a little more time.

What must it be like to leave this life when we have notice? How hard, or easy, is it to let go of the rich lifetime of material experiences and memories we leave behind? How heartbreaking is it to say goodbye to loved ones?

The will to live is strong. I saw this playing out in my dad's death, and I saw it playing out in Jamie.

THROUGHOUT THAT WEEKEND before the euthanasia appointment, Jamie continued to reach out. We brought his platform onto the bed with us at night. Jamie was right between our faces, as he had always loved to be. Somehow, Jamie found the strength to drag himself off the platform with his paws and legs. He snuggled closer to Chris, nestled under Chris's armpit.

"Why do we have these animals?" Chris pleaded. My husband's heart was being broken open, again and again—made better with pain and love.

I wasn't in much better shape. That week, on a tele-class with ten people from around the world who I barely knew, I burst into tears and sobbed loudly over the phone.

Jamie purred loudly all night long in the bed. He seemed strangely happy. He was using every moment he could. Did he know the exact moment of death? Did he know about the euthanasia appointment?

As had become the tradition, Jamie pawed repeatedly at Chris's face at 4:00 a.m. in the morning. "Time to eat," he was saying. "Time to get up." Move on, move on.

Monday came.

But Jamie was alert and engaged with the world. He still did not seem to be in pain. He was very hungry. He swatted at and knocked over a fourteen-ounce can of cat food. He stuck his paw in it. If he could eat by himself, he would have done so. He followed me with his eye. I looked closely at his eye for dilation, a sign of systems shutting down, but I didn't see it.

My first cat, Tigger, died at home. The night before she died, her eyes dilated and she got wobbly on her legs. Jamie's eye was clear and full of will. I did not want to take him to the vet, and I knew the local vet was probably too busy to come here. And it didn't seem time. Not yet. Chris and I agreed.

I called the vet and cancelled the appointment. I told Beth, the wonderful vet tech who taught me how to give subcutaneous fluids, that it seemed that Jamie wanted to pass on at home, his way. This, of course, completely fit Jamie. Jamie wanted everything his way.

A memory pushed into my awareness. Tiny Jamie, a three-week old kitten we'd just brought home from the pet store in St. Paul. Tiny Jamie in the bedroom, a kitten who was hardly bigger than the palm of my hand. Tiny Jamie clawing his way up a full-sized bed, including mattress and box spring. Tiny Jamie settling in near our heads with a self-satisfied look and a wall-rattling purr. I have never forgotten that drive of Jamie's.

We brought him into the bed, as usual, on Monday night. We placed his cardboard platform near our heads. He purred loudly and continuously, just as he did that first time so many years ago. Jamie was greedy in his need to be with us and love us. We greedily accepted. All three of us gave everything we could. Something had formed and continued to form between the three of us. It was will, powered by unconditional, continuous and strong love. At times like these—though I was completely on edge and felt as if I was falling off a cliff—I felt I might be approaching purity or what was is to be a good human being. I might be loving completely, unconditionally, and fearlessly.

NIGHT TIME.

Dimly, through foggy sleep, I was aware of a paw. Pressure on my hand.

Jamie was near my head. He was reaching for my hand with his paw. Gently, with claws barely out, Jamie hooked his paw over my hand. Gently, he drew my hand toward him. He wanted me to touch him and keep my hand on him. I held my hand on him and drifted in and out of sleep. If my hand strayed away while I slept, Jamie gently grabbed it back and brought it close to him. This went on all night. I held my hand on him; if my hand drifted away when I fell back asleep, he pulled it back to him. We were connected; we were treasuring every inch, every second, every moment of our connection. We were walking through the long stretch together.

TUESDAY.

Chris went to work. Jamie was alert. He was up; his eye was bright and not dilated. He watched me constantly, eye following me wherever I was. I put him with me, as I moved through our house. The bonus of having an extremely small house is that I was never far from Jamie. I wanted Jamie to have the reassurance I was there. I wanted him never to be alone. It seemed he was treasuring the connection, and I would do my best to keep the connection strong. I treasured it in a way I never thought possible.

I readied the canned food to feed Jamie. He smacked the heavy can again, knocking it over. He was so hungry. I would wonder, later, whether I should have pursued a feeding tube for him. Was I a coward about what other people would think? Would the university veterinary hospital have put a feeding tube in a cat this old?

I started to feed Jamie, syringing food into his throat as usual. And something changed. He began to gurgle.

"Okay, okay," I said, still not realizing what was coming. "We'll stop."

I picked him up, and held him. He flopped against my shoulder. Oh no. Oh no. Part of my mind grasped it, part didn't. "Oh no, honey." I held him, tears streaking down my face. "Let's go outside!" I wasn't making sense. I was holding him, petting him, telling him I loved him. I sped out the door with him, carrying him through the yard, hoping he could feel the soft summer breeze he loved. "Jamie Tuega. Jamie Tuega," I whispered. I talked. I sang his songs to him. I held him. I brought him back into the house, not knowing what propelled me, simply acting as if something else, something bigger, was directing me. I didn't know when he actually passed. Maybe there was never a time. Maybe this was drawn out, too. Maybe Jamie was hanging on. How could I love so much? How could we all love so much and go through this again and again? I set him down on the table and I sat down, my tears falling, moving in a dream, his face close to mine. His eye was dilated. I saw slowly, so slowly, the fire and the will leaving the eye. Where did it go? Where did such will go?

JAMIE, MY SWEETHEART.

Jamie, I cannot let you go.

I would never understand this. Could we ever understand it?

How can you be there and then be gone? How can the will of life be there, then gone? I have seen it before, I had been with it before; with my dad and with my friend the artist, with Tigger and Cleo and three dogs. But I was no closer to understanding it. I could not wrap my human mind around death. How could someone be there and gone? Where does their essence go?

DURING THAT TIME, I didn't move from the table. I stroked Jamie. I talked to him. I sung his songs. I told him how wonderful he was. I couldn't believe he was there, but not there. When I couldn't bear the grief, I checked email obsessively to zone out.

Sensitive Kieran picked up on something. He jumped on the chair next to me, but seemed more concerned about me than about Jamie.

I punched Chris's work number into my cell phone.

Chris did not answer his work phone. I left a message on his voice mail, hung up, and waited. He did not call.

I wondered why the cats always died when I was the only one home. Tigger, Target, now Jamie. What was the deal? I touched Jamie's smooth orange fur. He still seemed alive, but very still. He was not cold or stiff yet.

I finally called Chris again. I think I was afraid for Chris's heart. We must all go through grief but somehow, I wanted to protect my husband. I feared his heart might be more tender than mine.

Chris answered.

"Did you get my message?"

"What message?"

I told Chris what happened.

"Let me shut the door," he gasped, and I heard a sob in his throat. I pictured him getting up quickly in his office forty-five miles from our home, closing the door so no one would see him lose his composure. My heart broke for him.

"What happened?"

I told him, recounting everything. We were both talking through tears.

Chris headed home so we could both be with Jamie. The rest of the day was quiet, heavy, tearful, funny with memories, respectful, loving—all these contradictory things that float around the mystery of death.

Aftermath

Jamie, I miss you so much. I still can't believe you're gone. I want contact. I want to feel your head against mine in the bed. I want to hear your purr; I want to feel your paw tapping me or scraping me on the cheek.

No one slept with me last night. Chris was in the Boundary Waters Wilderness and I missed him. I hoped he was doing his own grieving and even more so, I hoped he connected with Jamie.

I so wanted to walk with ease in this other reality. When I "felt" Jamie in the woods, or in the yard; when I felt that quiet presence that was hard to explain—was this the other reality? It almost sounded like someone talking about God, but for me, I was talking about cats.

I reassembled the bed and put it back on the frame. When Jamie began to weaken and jumping suddenly wasn't going so well for him, we put the mattresses on the floor so he could get on and off the bed easily. The bed was a place that Jamie loved.

I cried on and off throughout the day. This was pretty typical but I worried I was starting to be numb. This grief was too much. I wanted more quiet time, so I could hear, so I could see Jamie between the spaces of breath, moments, time. I still couldn't get my head around that I'd never have him in his animate body again. I was way too attached to the body. This never failed to surprise me since I don't think of myself as a materialistic person. But I am—I have an attachment to the material form.

I drove to Ely and got myself a massage. I had decided to practice good self care this weekend—Jamie's hospice care was one of the most demanding things I'd ever done. I know people go through this with parents all the time. *What is wrong with me?* said the distorted part of my brain—the part that wanted to convince me I was crazy. But I knew there was nothing wrong with me—we all grieve in our own way.

On the road to Ely, Emmylou Harris sang a song about a black boy who was murdered in Mississippi for looking at a white woman. It was chilling, detailed song, and next to that song, my problems seemed small—but no less real.

Dyson curled against my leg as I wrote on the bed. Kieran was sitting at my feet. Maybe now I would have cat company tonight. I still hoped Jamie visited. I was not sure what to look for and I hoped I was open enough to sense him if and when he crossed the veil to visit. And if he wanted to come back as a cat or kitten, that was fine, too.

I miss you, my cat full of will. I miss your softness, hidden under the persnickety. Why was this harder than losing a parent? I loved too much.

How could something so small and so powerful be gone? I missed Jamie's effort he put into everything:

Pawing.

Blowing in ears.

The last night.

Kisses on lips.

Yes, he kissed me right on the lips. I have never had a cat do this. He did it in one of those intense special moments during the last two months of his life.

Dyson slept on the bed with me, nuzzling and head butting the whole night. Was Jamie informing him? Was Dyson lonely? Or did it simply suddenly click in Dyson's head that here was a great bed-time loving opportunity?

I needed to call bookstores in San Francisco, and I didn't want to. I wanted a retreat, seclusion, to do nothing and have the money roll in. I wanted only to love my cats. That was all. I was best at that, so that was what I should do to make money! Why shouldn't the paradigm be different?

I attended a yoga class and cried when we sang a Sanskrit mantra for removing obstacles. It was the same mantra I sang to Jamie, along with his several songs.

There was no rush, I told myself. No rush to grieve, no rush to think Jamie would leave. Jamie was here. Jamie was everywhere. He was in the wind and blue skies. He was in the yard. He was in the sound of the leaves. He was in the soft moss under my knees when I kneeled to pick the berries. He was on the bed, though I had not seen him. There was no hurry. That was the wisdom I felt. Where he was—in the other reality I wanted to know—there was no shortage of time, and rushing made no sense. I wondered if there was any bond more tender than that of a person and an animal companion.

I hoped tonight for insightful dreams. I hoped for the touch of Jamie's head close to mine, for a head butt, for a paw on the face, for a tender moment that transcended communication.

A SNIPPET OF AN IMAGINARY conversation popped into my mind:

Friend: "You look different."
Me: "All the layers have been peeled away. The grief mask-peel. There's nothing here but me."

I would probably never talk to a friend like this, but it was interesting how the honesty and directness came through for me internally. Grief did this. It polished me like a diamond, leaving the best and most beautiful parts of me—I hoped.

My mind whirled in circles until grief temporarily took it down. Chris was supposed to come out of the Boundary Waters Wilderness today. What if he didn't come out? What if he didn't want to come home? I needed to process with him. "HOLM," I almost wrote. What if he didn't want to go camping with *me* in two days?

I did yoga and meditated on the deck in the morning. It was a little late—10:00 a.m.—and already getting quite hot. I sweated in the heat thrown off the south side of the house. I felt very close to Jamie.

I did feel closer to him outside. We were having beautiful weather, and I felt Jamie all around me in the wind, the sky, the deck, the picnic table where he loved to lie in the past two months and be with us when we were eating. We fed him tiny morsels of meat because he so missed tasting food, and though he couldn't get it down, he enjoyed the taste. It was harder on Chris than me to watch this. I thought we were offering Jamie enjoyment, no matter how strange. Chris thought it was a struggle for Jamie. We saw it differently.

Would Chris talk to me about Jamie when he came home from camping? Would he go back into the woods with me on Wednesday?

When I meditated on the deck, I imagined Jamie's head close to mine. He loved close proximity to our heads—head butting, riding on shoulders, blowing in ears. This was a big deal to him.

In my meditation, Jamie told me what I already knew:

"I am everywhere."

I didn't have to imagine him in my lap. He could be on my lap and on my shoulders at the same time. It was a strange other reality we don't often inhabit in this material world, but somehow, it made sense.

I hoped Chris would let me cry in front of him. I needed to grieve too. We all do, and we have no control over how it comes out. I think it is fruitless to try and control it.

Tigger was so obviously a butterfly. Milo sent a shooting star. Target showed up as a big cat head via an antique red pitcher we have. What was Jamie? If I saw the words Tuega, or Little Train, or Dry Tortugas, or Laredo, or Tuega Time, I would know. These were parts of Jamie's songs. Months later, I was insanely happy when I spotted an RV on the highway called "Laredo." I saw various "Laredo" RVs in the next several months.

Jamie was in the grass. Jamie had the energy of grass, on a day with a soft wind. This was and is Jamie's tender side, the side that came through so strongly in the last two intense months. Jamie was the wind when I walked in the woods. He was comforting me, riding my shoulders like a warm and soft shawl.

NEVER WAS THERE A CAT *that loved like Jamie*, I thought, but I'm not sure if this was really true or if my mind was muddled and exhausted by recent events. I felt I could sleep forever. I wished I had the money to get a weekly massage.

We did not know when Jamie was going to die, though in some low deep down place we didn't want to look at, we knew it was coming. I still railed and fought against this fact of life. Jamie knew it was coming, and he may have known the end time better than we did. Did he time it so Chris wouldn't be home? Did he make sure I was there? I had no warning.

Jamie pulled out all the stops to communicate. He *always* asked for what he wanted.

This morning, someone thanked me for asking for what I wanted.

Another Jamie lesson.

THE DAY OR TWO before Jamie died, I carried him around. He loved to be outside but he especially loved being held, and touching our bodies. As I carried him around our yard, he raised his head to my ear, and blew gently. Another Jamie gift.

How many people would notice? How many people would attach significance? I was beyond caring what anyone thought—I am who I am.

We are still pondering the lessons.

IT WAS HARD to get over this, although we were blessed with two wonderful months. Jamie pulled out every stop imaginable. You think you know everything about love, and then you go through something like this. You learn love can be boundless. There is no scarcity of love—it is the most abundant thing in the Universe. It is as freeing as it is heartbreaking. It is equally joyous, saving, liberating, horrible, tiring, unforgettable—all of it. It is a mystery. We can only rub against the edges of it with our words.

I STILL COULDN'T BELIEVE Jamie was gone, and I knew concretely, like the slam of a heavy door, that he was gone. Again, it was one of those dichotomies around death. I couldn't believe Jamie didn't want to come back. He tried so hard to hang on. What was he doing now, and where was he? Was he missing us as much as we were missing him? I liked to believe in the Rainbow Bridge. I liked to imagine all my beloved animals would be waiting for me, across the bridge, when I passed over. Did Jamie want to come back? Could he come back?

Friends of mine have stories of how a beloved animal has "come back" as another animal. In some cases the resemblances have been uncanny. One friend had prophetic dreams that led her to pick out a kitten. She believed the kitten was her previous cat coming back into a new life. Another friend lost a dog, and through amazing circumstances, randomly came in contact with a new dog. Both dogs looked alike and had remarkably similar personalities.

I missed Jamie. I wanted him to come back. At the same time, I hesitated. We had our hands, and finances, full with five cats. We were the type that would spend money on expensive cat food, and expensive treatments, if the money was available. (Chris joked that we've funded our veterinarians' retirements.) Some would call us crazy. Others, such as my niece and her partner, were like us. These animals were squarely part of our family.

I COULD NOT MAKE myself go into my office.

My office was Jamie's favorite place, as was our bed. Jamie got loads of office time during the last two months of his life, and he loved it. I tried a few times to meditate there and I burst into tears. I was afraid to do yoga *asana* (the yoga postures). Yoga movement would unleash a grief I feared. I didn't want to feel that depth of grief—I was exhausted already from the grief I had been processing. There was a pile of stuff on the office floor—old files, paperwork, etc.—that needed to be put away or shredded. But I couldn't bring myself to move the stuff. It would be like moving on. I took my laptop and worked in the house.

Sometime in the days after Jamie passed, I emailed the vets and the vet tech, and told them. They sent me kind and compassionate responses. Jamie was blessed to live in our house, one said. He received excellent, compassionate treatment. I was grateful to hear this and it meant a lot to me.

It felt as if Jamie was in the office waiting for me to move on, to acknowledge him and at the same time, to let him go. Another one of those incomprehensible dichotomies around death. How can we ever understand it? We are human, we are of this life, we are here on earth. How can we ever truly comprehend passing over until we make that journey ourselves?

I LOOKED FOR, and waited for, a sign. Other cats have passed over and left me plenty of signs they are around. But not from Jamie. I wondered if he gave us everything he had. I wondered if he used up his allowance of love—if an allowance of love can ever be exhausted.

I took out Jamie's pictures when I was able to handle it.

Chris was not ready. "Don't do that," he said, "you'll drive yourself crazy."

But I needed to look at those pictures. I needed to remember Jamie. I didn't want to forget, and I was afraid life and its demands would press in, and Jamie would become less real and more like a cutout, or an outline of a memory, or a faint sketch on tracing paper, and soon he would be gone. I studied the photos; laughing, crying. Jamie snuggled up on a cane chair with Milo when we first moved up to northern Minnesota. Jamie as a tiny kitten, looking up into the camera, his orange fur clashing with the oddly patterned white-and-brown linoleum of our old apartment kitchen floor. And three professional shots of Jamie. I was so glad I spent the money, several years ago, to have these shots taken by an exceptional photographer in Ely. I would treasure them forever. My favorite was a photo of Jamie half sitting, looking out rather than at the camera. His paws looked small under his chest. It reminded me of a benevolent king. An eight-by-eleven framed copy of that photo stared at me now, on the left side of my computer desk.

In the days or weeks after Jamie's passing, I had two dreams.

In the first dream, Two Day showed up at our house, followed by a gray, tabby, one-eyed kitten. Both were friendly. It didn't occur to me until I woke up that the one-eyed kitten might represent Jamie.

In the second dream, I was at a party. The location was a nice, well-furnished home surrounded by woods. There was a friendly feeling about the place and about the people. A cat weaved through and around people's legs, and came up to me. It was Jamie, and he had a white-ish aura, even though I knew he was orange. I couldn't take my eyes off his brilliant white. It was more than light. It was something bigger but there was not language for it—at least not language I knew. I had a deep knowing that this was Jamie, and he was happy and had come to be with me.

Later, I would remember I dreamt of a brilliant white mountain lion after Tigger died. It was this same sort of white brilliance that Jamie exuded in this dream. Jamie had both eyes in the dream.

I held him in the dream and he was very real. I could feel his fur and his warmth; his purr and his whiskers tickled my forearms. That moment went beyond dream and into that place where dreams felt like real life. Jamie was clearly communicating from wherever he was. *I'm okay. I love you. Our bond is too strong to be broken.* And that mirrored how I felt. Our bond was so strong, too strong to be broken.

Two months after Jamie passed, I went into the office.

I sat on the floor. I pulled the paper shredder close to me. The office was tiny and paper on the floor took up a lot of room. I needed to make space for Jamie. I needed to make space to take the next step. Moving on? Simply living? I didn't know what I call it—I knew that it was time.

I shredded old paper that needed to go. There was something very comforting about this thoughtless, mechanical activity. I was cleaning up. Jamie would be pleased. There would be space in the office for me again and for him. Maybe he would come and sit on my shoulders, like a feline scarf, as I worked. Maybe I'd feel his weight on my shoulders or hear his rumbling purr. Maybe out of the corner of my eye I'd glimpse him curled up on my yoga mat, soaking up the sun through a large southern window.

Hours and hours later the paper was gone, shredded to bits, and placed in a large bag to be taken to recycling.

I meditated, breathing my thanks to Jamie Tuega. I cried, but I held relief in my heart. I had let the office back into my life, and with it, Jamie.

Jamie, stalking his prey.
(Courtesy of Deborah Sussex Photography.)

Catherine Holm

"Why Do We Have These Animals?"

During the long goodbye we were honored to experience with Jamie, Jamie did many endearing things we will never forget. Many of these were mannerisms I had never seen from Jamie before. One night as we both lay in bed, Jamie crawled into the crook of Chris's armpit. This completely unhinged Chris, and I could see my husband trying not to cry. Grief is especially hard for Chris, who has difficulty expressing it.

"Why do we have these animals, anyway?" he said. "They just break your heart."

So true.

We can easily say these experiences forge us into stronger people, but they are still not easy to go through. Jamie was weakening at this point. We'd put him on the bed, though Chris wanted him to stay on my side. But with the strength Jamie had, he dragged himself over to Chris. I think Jamie wanted to be sure that goodbyes and tenderness were spread evenly and equally between us. I believe he did a good job.

Why do we go through this?

It is the worst kind of hurt imaginable. I can only imagine that it must be similar to losing a child. I don't have human children, so I will never have that experience.

Does the joy of having and loving the animal through their lifetime outweigh the pain of losing the animal companion? I think so. As one friend said, "Do the math! Twenty years of love versus two weeks of pain." Insert your own numbers. In most cases, you get a lot more quality life time with your animal companion than you get of the tough illness and grieving time. Thank the gods.

How sterile it would seem to come home to a house without animals. How I would miss their distinct personalities. Each cat and dog has their own stories, and hopefully, a life that has been honored by us as much as possible. We have songs we sing for each cat, a myriad of nicknames that make no sense to anyone but that make us laugh, books that have been inspired by these animals. We have laugher and playtime.

Rama (a.k.a. Dyson), for example, is my current black cat. Dyson loves to play a game where I drag a sheet on the floor. He'll attack the sheet, riding it as I drag him around. It never fails to make me laugh.

My husband shakes his head. "This is a nuthouse," he'll say, but he's smiling as he says it. He loves to watch Dyson play, too. What better mood lifter during a long cold winter?

Watching Chester play with his "baba" is great entertainment. Chester carries the baba around and drops it at our feet. Better yet, he leaves it in very strategic places where we will find it—the center of the door threshold, or on the bed at bedtime, or right outside the bathroom door when one of us is in the bathroom and about to come out. Clever cat, that Chester. He's learned to stand by the baba and howl determinedly until we get the idea and throw it for him.

Kieran makes us laugh with his antics—he loves music. If Chris pulls out the guitar, Kieran is instantly on his lap. Kieran listens and seems to like the vibrations of music. When Chris starts to play, Kieran stares into the sound hole on the body of the guitar, fascinated with the sound and the innards of the instrument. When I play piano, he jumps on the keys to help me out. I have a friend who is an accomplished pianist, but when she watched our cats, Kieran showed no interest in her piano playing. If Chris and I are making music, iyl;t's a whole different story.

The world is crazy and complicated. The news can get us down if we let it. We all face our mortality, especially as we get older. Change happens and we may have no control. The simple love and joy of an animal companion is a salve for life. Happiness starts at home, whatever the situation.

These are good things to remember when we start fearing the heartbreak, and start asking ourselves, "Why do we have these animals?"

Wilderness Healing

WHEN I NEED TO HEAL, I have always gone into nature. Nature's quiet can get me to that peaceful place where I can grieve, be still, and empty my tired brain.

When Target died, we headed for the Vermont mountains.

After Jamie's passing, we headed for the Boundary Waters Wilderness.

True, we had made the reservation months before. We were to go into the BWCA on the Gunflint side, which I hadn't paddled in thirty years. It is much easier for us to go in on the Ely side. The Gunflint side is a three-and-a-half-hour trip away, and involves an overnight the day before you put in to the wilderness. If Jamie had continued to live, Chris would have taken the trip alone. We'd hoped for that outcome, actually.

I've thought a lot lately about optimism and denial, of the fortitude to keep going. Jamie kept going, and going, and going, and because he was so obviously enjoying life until the last minute, we never lost hope. It was a strange simultaneous feeling of knowing that death was near and being ready, yet not ever ready. Even when Jamie could no longer walk, I hoped the kidney supplements (which arrived too late) would help. I never did find out if muscle wasting is reversible. Almost two weeks after Jamie's death, I couldn't imagine how we did all the care.

We are all amazing when we're pushed to extremes. Was I the eternal optimist? Or deeply in denial? It sure felt more like the energy of optimism rather than that of denial. And Jamie was having fun too. He used every resource to keep communicating.

For our Gunflint Boundary Waters trip, we car camped at Iron Lake, a campsite about ten miles from where we would put in to the wilderness the next morning. The area had been burned in a huge fire in 2007. Charred tree trunks stood among popple underbrush that was beginning to grow back. Berries love a burned out area, and berries were everywhere—chokecherries, raspberries, a few blueberries, and a huge variety of raspberry I have never seen. (I ate one before realizing it wasn't the raspberry I am used to seeing, but had no ill effects.)

The light at this time of August was just beginning to change. The quality of the light, with the burned out and open landscape, gave the campground a surreal feel. There were only seven campsites at Iron Lake, and they were mostly empty. We cooked a meal and got ready for the trip the next morning. Car camping has never gotten into my soul the way wilderness camping does.

Jamie was in my soul. I needed to remember that. But it was a different reality. And it took some getting used to.

The next morning, we woke early, eager to get into the real wilderness. We put in at Round Lake, and took a few short portages into Brandt Lake, where we set up camp. On Round Lake, we got turned around a little and had to consult the map to find the right portage. When we did land at the correct portage, a black-and-white butterfly greeted us and led the way. This happened over and over again during this trip.

I knew when I first saw the black-and-white butterflies that this would be one form of Jamie. It made sense to me that Jamie would come as a snarlier butterfly. Tigger was the soft and gentle cat and would come as a yellow butterfly. Jamie would be white-and-black, or blue-and-brown.

Of course, these cats always fooled us and became more than they were toward the end of their lives. In the last two months, Jamie's persnickety-ness dropped away. Tenderness I didn't know any of us were capable of (Chris, I, or Jamie) grew and grew and grew.

At the Brandt Lake campsite, where we camped for three days, I picked berries and wrote poetry to Jamie:

Where You Are

Jamie, where you are, is it cold, is it hard?
Jamie, do you long for the pressure of my arms?
Jamie, when can I hold my head next to yours again?
Jamie, how can I understand this place beyond the dreams?
Mother, where I am is hard to capture in your words
Mother, you are holding me and I am with you now
Mother, know that all is one and one is all
Mother, in this place the heart is king and not the head
Jamie, there is pain and there is love and there is hope
Jamie, when the tears have emptied me and what is left,
Jamie, what is left I cannot ever know
Jamie, what is left I'll have to dive deep to see
Mother, here there is no pain and all is turned to joy
Mother, hold me close and travel deep into my heart
Mother, we have forever and we have it everywhere
Mother, knowing this will ease your life and soothe your heart
Mother, travel in and bury first your face in fur
Rest your cheek upon mine and gaze into my eye of green
And know that there is more and so much more but start here
now
And stroke my tail and scratch my cheek and let me lay a paw
Upon your hand and I will gently pull your hand toward me
And you will come and you will come into that other place
And here we'll stand and both be everywhere because we're all
And you will know that separation ends and now we're free
And love will fill our hearts and we will merge in greatest joy
To know what could not be until the time was right for us
The mountain lion running down the hill was not for me
The mountain lion running down the hill was sent for you
So muster courage now and open heart and love comes
through
And know that all goes on and I am with you through and
through
And love this way with open heart and let the world know
YOU.

Catherine Holm

I also wrote this poem:

To Anyone Who Has Ever Gone

Are you dwelling in the cracks
At the bottom of my heart
Are you shining in the sun
When the rays caress my face
Are you living in the dirt
Bonding gently to bare feet
Are you swimming toward my heart
In the ripples of the lake
Can the bond between us hold
Heart to heart a golden cord
Water soft and ever strong
Will I know your song at night
Will you come to me in dreams
In the soft voice of the wind
Can I hold you for this time
Stretch it out into beyond
Can I know you in this place
Where all boundaries cease to be
Can my heart envelope yours
In an everlasting peace
I can know you in the wind
In the burnt branch of a tree
In the flutter of the wing
Of a black/white butterfly
We can know this if we try
In this world of edge and endings
You will seep into my heart
Endless pure clean watershed
And the day I cease to be
I will merge with all my loves

In a strengthened unity
That I've had a glimpse of here
Are you watching through the cracks?
Guide me close, o being passed on
So someday I'll understand
Of the greatness we can be
I will see it in the sun
In the glance of sparkled wave
In the pause between the wind
And I'll know that you are there.

THE QUIET OF NATURE was healing. I didn't always want to be rushing off somewhere else. I wanted to be still to notice the glitter of the water. To see the sun come up. To watch the sky quickly deepen with stars. To find a patch of berries. To wander slowly and start at the formations of underbrush.

Jamie, I felt far from your physical form. I was not sure what this meant. Had you moved on? I still could not believe the power and immensity of your love for us. No one would believe me when I told them the details. They would think I was delusional with grief or denial. Why should I care?

Jamie, are you there in the wave sound of the wind
Jamie are you hiding in the cool and rocky depths
Jamie are you berries bursting forth with brilliant blue
Are you the lap of water at the rock and grassland shore
Are you the sun from clouds
Peeking forth to cast your warmth
Are you the heart of ours
Breaking open to the world
Are you in Chris's arm, nestled close as you can get
Is your head pressed close to mine in the whisper of the wind?

Jamie, curled up on a warm, fluffy bed.
(Courtesy of Deborah Sussex Photography.)

Letting Go

I don't think letting go is easy for many of us. As far as animal companions go, I feel as if I'm becoming an expert. In the last two years, five cats and dogs have passed on at our household. Every journey is a bit different. But one similarity remains through it all—again, I'm faced with letting go.

Since I believe I'll meet them all again someday over the Rainbow Bridge, I don't know why letting go should be such an issue. The thing is, I get so attached to their FORM. How they feel, how they look, the sound of their purrs, the pressure of their paws on my lap, their unique personalities, and the funny things they do. And when they're gone, there's a hole.

If I could get past this business of form, how much less suffering and grieving there'd be around death.

I have found myself preparing when I know one of my companions is nearing the end of life. I begin to imagine (to myself) how it will be without that companion. I used to try to avoid these thoughts, but I've come to recognize them for what they are—my strategy for moving through the grieving process.

The Yoga tradition has as one of its ethical guidelines the principle of non-possessiveness. We can't truly possess anything and everything will eventually return to formlessness. Every time an animal companion departs from my life, hurtful as it may be, it is also a huge gift that can teach me about the rest of life. What am I holding to too tightly? What needs letting go?

And of course, it's a great lesson in living in the moment, loving your cat or dog or companion now. We have the present moment, not the past or the future. The present moment can be savored, loved, shared. My companions are always teaching me.

Why I Grieve So Hard

In what can feel like a cold and lonely world, my cats have been my ballast. They have been the friends who are always there for me. I wonder if I get more knocked off my center than others when an animal of mine passes. I know this can't be true. Grief is personal and a lot can be going on under the surface for another—depths I may not pick up on.

What's most interesting about this grief for me is that it brings a lingering feeling of aloneness. Where does this come from? Fortunately, I have my husband—a giving and caring person. I worry that I am too much for him. He struggles with his own demons. The cats play.

The cats bring play into a household that could turn far too serious, or sterile, otherwise.

When humans want to run from intimacy, animal companions push us into intimacy, forcing us to care for them, love them, play with them, feed them.

I am comforted by the insight that I can never be too much for my cats.

They're much like dogs that way. I can be as outrageous as possible. I can demand love, and they will meet me where I need to be met.

Some people may disparagingly suggest that the cats fill a void that children should be filling. I have never mothered human children. Is the loss of a pet as bad as the loss of a child? I am betting there are similar depths of grief. Most parents hope they don't outlive their children. All of us with animal companions know we will probably outlive our companions. It's something I am never ready for, even though I've been through it many times.

We differ in how we treat humans and animals at the end of life. We'll provide all kinds of life support for humans, but easily pull the plug for an animal. Often the action is driven by practicality or financial considerations. Some would look at me and say I treat my animals too much like humans. But I should stop worrying about what others say—it only clutters my mind more.

I picked berries in late summer with my girlfriend in a swampy area surrounded by spruce. August light filtered through the trees. Her golden retriever sat on the sphagnum moss, his soft reddish fur a contrast to the greens of the plant life and the soft dusk that indicates the beginning of a transition from summer into fall. We talked about one theme that is common through all spiritual beliefs—the ability of deep grief to open the heart and to help us experience profound and tender love. That is what I felt—it was as if my heart was evolving to love at new levels. I grabbed onto the familiar —the feel of berries in my hand, my thumb gently brushing the fruit off tiny stems, berries falling into my pail. This was familiar. But grief is an expedition, with twists and turns and surprises.

In my most distorted moments, I wonder who will take care of me when I die. Will anyone be around who cares? Could there be a fate worse than dying in a nursing home? I think not. Will I have the chance to check out from life myself, if the nursing home looms as the only option? These are horrible, unhappy thoughts I try not to have. I know some of these have been spurred on by Jamie's death, and some of it is spurred on by the fact that I am in the second half of life. Another friend is contemplating separation from her partner. The eighty-year-old neighbor just died. Two of my high school classmates died this year (too young).

I tell myself, and I hope: Jamie lives on.

His energy is everywhere, manifested through black and white butterflies and dragonflies.

When I die, will people see *me* as butterflies? Will there be anyone left who knows me?

When I've been outside, and if Jamie flits into my thoughts, the butterfly is there, suddenly, flying near my face. This happens all day. I always thank Jamie. Dragonflies have flown straight into Chris. Dragonflies have kissed Chris. Chris sees it too. The smoke alarm in the house went off, reminding me of our travels after Target died and a smoke alarm in an upstate New York motel that wouldn't quit and sounded just like Target.

I love you, Jamie. I still get teary. Certain parts of the yard bring up emotions—the places where you liked to hang out. I will spend some time with your energy. Because that is what you are now, energy—and you are everywhere.

I SAT IN MY OFFICE, on my yoga mat, facing a *mandala* that I created on a cardboard circle at a transformative workshop. The *mandala* captures, in words and pictures, my dreams for my life. It sits upright on the floor, propped by the wall behind it. Above it, an old paned window looks out into our woods of aspen, birch, spruce, and balsam.

Here, in this place, I could not run from the memories of you, Jamie. You always sat in the green rocking chair, watching me. Or you came over to the mat and laid next to my feet. I looked at the green chair and you were not there, yet you were.

A *mandala* painted by my deceased artist friend portrays Tigger and hangs on the wall above the green chair. And if I looked straight ahead on the makeshift altar that has never been formally acknowledged as an altar, your hair was placed inside mala beads that are strewn in an informal circle. Crow Woman, a small paper mache figurine given to me, was on her back. She needed to be fixed and her feet needed to be glued back to her legs.

Why are we so afraid of the silence, Jamie? That is where the mysteries are, in the quiet. I go there every day in meditation. Meditating in the office, that was a different story. Because you were, and are, there.

The office was your passion. You loved to be there because you could have your own domain. You could be the only cat and you were a totally different cat in the office—much less snarky, more affectionate and loving.

And in this respect, you outdid yourself in your last two months on the earth. You loved in a way we had never seen. You never wanted the bond to be broken.

Chris told me he has the feeling you will come back, Jamie, if I want it badly enough. I don't want to force you back.

I have known a few people who have had near-death experiences, and my deceased artist friend was one of these people. Apparently what they experience on the other side is wonderful. Some don't want to come back. Is that where you are, Jamie?

I will not force you back, but I miss you. I miss your quiet and sweet way. It was the thing in you I always knew; the thing Chris did not see. Chris got distracted with your snarkiness. Another lesson? There are too many to keep track of.

Thoughts About the End of Life

We think nothing about extending the life of humans through every means possible. Things get trickier when it comes to animal companions. What is right? What is wrong?

Animals cannot tell us if they are suffering, and that is one of the big differences between human and animal care at the end of life. With cats, it is even trickier. Cats have evolved to hide their suffering. This is a survival mechanism.

Was Jamie suffering? We watched carefully and struggled with the decision every day. What made us keep going with the palliative care was the way Jamie showed us he was still engaged and interested in living. His eye never lost its brightness or determination. He continued to have fun and engage in life.

Was I selfish to give this cat two more months? Did I do it simply to fill my bottomless need for the love from my cat? I don't know. I do know that he seemed to be enjoying it. Jamie wanted to stretch out the goodbye just as much as we did. I am not sure he wanted to go. He knew what was coming, and he made every second count. I believe Jamie wanted to die on his own terms, at home, with us—and that is what he got.

The decision to provide palliative care versus euthanizing a companion animal is complicated. What is quality of life and when does the quality go downhill? When is that blurry line crossed? These are tough questions. Is it complicated in my household because the cats are essentially my "kids"? It may be. Would the cats hold less of a priority in my life if I had children? I don't know and I will not get the opportunity to find out in this lifetime. I'm not anticipating having children.

Sometimes my drive with cats—my life with cats—seems to be an exercise in courage, and sometimes it feels like a lesson in experiencing how many different ways our companions get to leave this life. The grief stays strong during each of these experiences. I had hoped it would get easier over time.

I need, instead, to focus on the joy and the gifts our animal companions bring. I need to remember that Jamie kissed me on the lips days before his death, and that he blew in my ear, and that he loved the office and that I can still feel him in there. I need to give them the best life I possibly can, and help them gently, kindly, courageously, and wisely, through the inevitable final passage.

Stretching

THE PROCESS OF SAYING goodbye is a lot like stretching. Jamie's death made me aware of this, and it also made me aware of how hard it is for me to accept change. The latter was an eye opener. I like to think of myself as a flexible person—up for adventure and willing to swing with whatever life throws at me. That's an attractive picture (or delusion)—a woman who can handle what life dishes out. But nothing destroys that delusion faster for me than the health issues or impending death of a beloved animal companion. Then I discover I'm really a mess. I can't handle change at all. Grief brings me to my knees. The power of it is humbling.

The older I've gotten, the more opportunities I've had to stretch into a lot of new situations. That's not a bad thing—in fact, I usually feel good after each situation, even though I can have great trepidation beforehand. Stretching was on my mind when I read from my short story collection to people I didn't know, shortly after Jamie's death. Of course I have done this before, and it always went well. But this particular reading was in California and not on "my turf," whatever that is.

I knew it would not matter in the least. I'd do the readings and they would go well. Wasn't the whole world my turf? And where does the concept of turf come from, anyway? Feudal infighting? Land-holding? Cook, Minnesota, has certainly not always (ever?) felt like my turf, so why should I be any more concerned about San Francisco?

Jamie was a turf-y kind of cat. He loved being in the office and that was his turf. Jamie thrived on attention and that was never more apparent than when he was in the office. There I could do things with him that I could never get away with in the house. I could brush him without him objecting. He would climb into my lap and nuzzle and purr. Directed affection really brought out the tender side of Jamie. He loved to sit on the green rocking chair and watch me. From the chair, in my tiny office (sixteen feet by sixteen feet) Jamie could clearly see me, whether I worked at my computer, or whether I meditated or did asana on my yoga mat.

Jamie stretched his time out with us, making the most of daily opportunities to connect with us, be with us, and show us his love. If only I could live (and love) so mindfully and fully.

Chris, much more the atheist than I am, surprised me in how he dealt with the death of Jamie. Chris believes our animals continue to exist in some form, and that where they go after death is much more fun than being here. Chris believes that we could hold our animals, and our mutual love for them (and theirs for us), in our hearts, and that they could live in our hearts forever.

Somehow, I was coming to know this was true.

It reminded me of seeing the psychic Sylvia Browne on a talk show, years ago. She stated that there was no "hell"—and that "hell" was this life we live here. I don't think she meant that in an entirely negative way—I think she was trying to say that where we go afterwards is much more joyous and glorious than we could ever hope to understand or attain in this limited, mortal lifetime and in our physical bodies. We may get glimpses of such bliss—what yoga calls *Samadhi*. But we are not yet the containers that can hold such bliss or such awareness and knowing, effortlessly and all the time.

Perhaps the animals are such containers. Perhaps this is why animal psychics claim that our animal companions are much more matter-of-fact about death than we humans are—because the animals have been walking in bliss all along and they get it. They get what it is to be a truly actualized, loving, joyous being. And this is their greatest lesson for us, I believe—their capacity to show us a depth of love and joy we can try to attain.

Our Calling

WHEN IT COMES to my cats, I want them to live forever. I can never get enough of their love, their mannerisms, their tangible presence. And this gets me into trouble when they eventually leave, as they must.

It was three weeks since Jamie had passed. Dragonflies flew into my face. Butterflies sprang up suddenly in my path when I was walking. I felt Jamie's presence in my office. It was a different kind of reality—a new quality to the quiet, sometimes a rose-scented smell. A deep deep stillness, like the quiet voice of intuition.

I wanted more, and I could not have more. I wanted Jamie back. How could such a bond be broken? How could such a strong bond ever end?

Spiritual people say the bond does not end. They believe the bond is never broken and we are always with our loved ones. Jamie was always in my heart. Jamie was everywhere. And sometimes I knew that.

And sometimes I still wanted more. I was a greedy human in these times, not a spiritual being. Jamie gave me twenty years of his life. Twenty years. A huge amount of time for any cat to be on the earth. Why couldn't I focus on his gift rather than his leaving? Why couldn't I thank him for his memories?

Jamie, a proud young cat with a plumy tail and pantaloons. Jamie, a tiny kitten no bigger than our hands. Jamie, when I found he had to have his eye removed. Me at the kitchen table, head in hands, crying, my heart so heavy I thought I might never get up. *I had let Jamie down*, I thought. *Never again.*

These animals walk through stuff a lot more gracefully than I can hope to imitate.

Jamie had been through many things in his life. Early onset kidney disease, which I think ultimately contributed most to his death. Risky eye surgeries at age eighteen. And his final process of passing—two months of intense three-way love (me, Chris, Jamie) and hospice at home. Jamie got what he wanted, and we gave it openheartedly, joyfully, tearfully.

Some people feel most spiritual in church, or aligning with a religion.

Some find spirit in nature. I am one of the latter.

But I have also felt at my spiritual best when I am caring for my animals, especially during tough times. I learn then that I am truly capable of love. That yes, I can love and nurture. Most people would look at me and laugh at that statement. "Of course you can nurture," they'd say, "you're one of the most gentle, nurturing people I know!" That may be what they see. And I guess that's good. But I worry about becoming numb, because this loving hurts too much.

If I had kids, maybe it'd be different. I never wanted kids—not strongly enough to make that very serious commitment. And so, I care for cats. I give them my heart. And they break my heart when they die.

Repeatedly.

Every death is different, full of surprises. It is the most challenging path I've ever walked, and it feels treacherous, sweet, horrid, wrenching, turn-inside-out—all at once.

As I wrote this section, Chester and Kieran wrestled on the floor —making a big thumping noise, which is always remarkable, given the small size of cats. Chester grabbed Kieran's head with his orange paws; Kieran's almost all-white body flopped down on the floor. They stared each other down—going through endless iterations of cat posturing. I was outside, writing. Sometimes the distance of glass or another building is needed. My cats can be demanding. They know how tuned in I am to them, and they know how good they've got it here.

When I wrote, this, I was going through some coach training in a new paradigm for helping people move through "mid-life crisis." My teacher preferred to call it "mid-life opportunity." Mid-life whatever was nothing new to me. The paradigm suggested that this transition often is laced with the desire to make more of a difference in the world. This transition came with the sense of moving beyond what we are, into something greater.

What is that for me? I think it has something to do with animal companions, and our relationship to them, and what they teach us. I have felt this strongly for a long time. How that helps the world, I am not sure. Perhaps the time is quickening, to find out.

Kali, the affectionate three-legged cat.
(Photo courtesy of the author.)

Epilogue

A LITTLE MORE than a year after Jamie passed on, I took my cat, Kali, to the veterinarian in Ely for a urinalysis. As I was paying my bill, the staff asked me if I wanted to see a kitten up for adoption. The clinic sometimes takes in strays to re-home. This kitten, they said, had been rescued in a nearby town and brought to the clinic by the cops. The cops were getting attached to her. The staff knew I would help spread the word about animals that needed a home.

I went with the staff into the holding room—the same place with so many memories, the same place where I started this story and wondered if I was saying goodbye to Jamie for the last time.

In a floor-level, stainless steel cage, a blue-gray tortoiseshell kitten stopped what she was doing. With orange eyes, the kitten gave me a look that felt older than her three months.

It felt as if she stared into my soul.

I froze, unable to break from her gaze.

"Wow," I said, finally, "that is one aware kitten."

I promised to get the word out to my email list, and asked the staff to send me a photo so I could post a notice on Facebook. I didn't think to take her out and hold her. The staff told me she was very precocious, and that she seemed unfazed by other cats and dogs in the holding room. She liked to cuddle and she was up-to-date on her shots.

I drove home, other thoughts and to-do lists and life filling my head. That night, I sent out notice of a gray kitten needing a home to everyone I could think of who might want a kitten, or might know other cat lovers. Then, I forgot about the kitten.

A few days later, our orange lily bloomed.

Chris had been in the habit of calling the flowers on this lily "Jamie flowers." The flowers were the color of Jamie. This lily had only ever bloomed in the spring. It never gets enough water, because it's under the south eave of the house and I forget to water it. We'd had an extremely dry summer. Chris and I took notice.

The same day, a blue-and-brown butterfly circled me many times when I stood on the patio next to the lily plant. The butterfly flew into my face.

I thought of the kitten, whose orange eyes had looked straight into my soul.

I remembered the first dream of Jamie I'd had after he passed. He'd shown up as a gray kitten with one eye. That was how I knew he was Jamie.

Slowly, I got the exciting feeling of gestalt, when things come together. I wondered at my ability to be so dense and not see things— me, who claimed to be so tuned in. How many other things had I not noticed?

Now was not the time to adopt, not with five cats who were doing quite well and getting along.

Still.

I called the clinic. The kitten waited for a home. We mulled over a decision.

One week later, with trepidation and excitement, I adopted the kitten and brought her home. On that day, the lily bloomed once more and the brown and blue butterfly flitted in circles around me again, on the patio, near the lily.

We named the kitten Jamie Bluebell.

Jamie Bluebell, the kitten sent by Jamie.
(Photo courtesy of the author.)

Karma (back) and Jamie Bluebell (front) relaxing in the hall.
(Photo courtesy of the author.)